247 Inspirational Ideas For Starting Your Own Home Business

Stuart Goldsmith

Copyright © Stuart Goldsmith 2002

First published in the United Kingdom by:
Medina Ltd, 230 Peppard Road, Emmer Green,
Reading, Berkshire, UK, RG4 8UA

First Published January 2002

Published by NS WebMarketing October 2021

All rights reserved. No reproduction, copy or transmission of this publication may be made without written permission. No paragraph of this publication may be reproduced, copied or transmitted without written permission, or in accordance with the Copyright Act 1956 (amended).

This book is sold for entertainment purposes only, and the author, publishers or distributors are not responsible for any actions taken as a result of reading this book.

What's This Book All About?

For over ten years I've been working with many aspiring entrepreneurs and business owners. The question I'm most often asked is: "I really want to get started, but I have no idea what to do! Can you give me some practical business ideas?"

The answer is 'Yes!' and here they are.

This book is divided into three parts:

1. **30 'Foolish' ideas which made their creators rich.** These are intended to inspire you. For the most part, these are ordinary men and women who just woke up one morning with a 'crazy' idea and wouldn't give up until they had made their dream a reality. In most cases, they have made very large sums of money (often in the millions) from these ideas. The purpose of this section is to make you think: "If he/she can do it, I know I can!" Also, the intention is to erase any negative thoughts you might have along these lines: "It's hopeless nowadays, everything's been done. Anyway, the little guy will never make any money, they'll see to that." Every day, people are bringing their winning ideas to market and retiring on easy street with big payoffs. Why not you? I'm also reminded of this true quote from the head of the UK patent office in 1899: "Everything which can be invented has already been invented." Yea.... right......

2. **30 realistic business ideas which you could operate right now.** Often these ideas are not keys to a fortune, but, they are ideas which are working out there, right now, making good money for people. You can use any one of these ideas for yourself, or give it a little twist or variation.

3. **187 'quick and simple' ideas**. The purpose of these ideas is to get your brain thinking. Often the ideas seem a bit crazy and unrealistic - almost too simple. But.... the intention is for these ideas to act as a trigger, making you say something like: "That idea's ridiculous, but if I change it around a bit I could..."

If you like this book, but can't find anything that inspires you to go out and start your own business, why not try **247 More Inspirational Ideas to Start Your Own Home Business**. You might just find the idea you need to set you on the road to success.

To be honest, if you're not looking for ideas around a particular type of business, but you do have a hobby or skill you're really passionate about, there's probably only 1 business I'd advise you to start. Its also ideal if you're on your own, have limited start up capital, or want to run it along side an existing job. Its a business where you can pursue your passion as well as earn a great living. So what would I recommend? Information Marketing. For a simple, effective, and profitable way to start in this lucrative business, take a look at **7 Sure-Fire Steps to a Successful Information Marketing Business**.

It's Never Been Easier To Start A Business!

There are more opportunities to start a business today than at any time during the history of mankind. There are six main reasons for this:

1) Many people today have a lot more leisure time and a high disposable income. This gives rise to a massive demand for hobbies, crafts, sports, games, amusements, holidays and weekend breaks.

2) Today's more competitive and diversified society means businesses and individuals are open to new ideas, services and products like never before. This creates a large potential market for training courses, educational aids, all kinds of information, specialised products and services, novelties, etc.

3) Anyone starting a business today has immense technology at his or her disposal including: computers, printers, photocopying machines, audio and video cassettes; audio and video recording equipment; low cost bulk printing; telephone answering machines, Internet and web sites etc. Twenty years ago the average multinational lacked the computing, communicating and printing power available to the ordinary person today.

4) Modern society demands its members have a lot of ability. In the course of a lifetime members are required to, for example:

* use a long list of consumer durables;
* fill out reams of forms;
* communicate with all kinds of people from advisors to workmen;
* complete complex transactions such as buying a house;
* sell himself/herself to potential employers, life partners, etc.;
* have opinions about everything from nuclear weapons to how local services should be run;

* run his/her life from managing personal finances to building a career.

All this is a far cry from the average 18th century person who was an illiterate farm labourer who never travelled more than four miles from home. This means that now the pool of potential business people is greater than ever before. If a person can live in modern society that person has the necessary ability to start a business.

5) More people have access to money than ever before. Until the late sixties most people were paid weekly and spent money as they earned it. Today most people have credit cards, which alone have spending limits equal to a half or full year's income. Savings and share holdings are greater than ever before. A large proportion of the population can raise money on their house. All this is underlined by the fact that more people and institutions are willing to lend money for a good business proposal.

6) Advice, courses and books about starting a business are within easy reach of everyone. There are also more helpful schemes organised by national and local government, private business and other groups.

What's Stopping You Starting?

As you can tell, its easier than ever to start your own business and more people are starting a business than ever before. But many more people are held back by two factors:

    1) the employee mentality, and
    2) most people have not developed their ability to generate business ideas.

Let's deal with each one in turn.

Employee Mentality:

There are many reasons why an employee should want to start a business but three are worth thinking about.

i) The difference between having your own business and having a job is the difference between buying a house and renting a house. If you rent a house you have all the satisfaction of living in a house, but at the end of the day you own nothing and can be evicted as quickly as you became a tenant. A job is just like a renting a house. However, your own business depends on you, because you are its owner, and at the end of the day it may leave you with considerable personal wealth.

ii) You are a unique person. The vast majority of employers do not recognise your uniqueness. Its said the universe is 14 billion years old and will last at least as long again. In all the time to come there will never be another person just like you. You are a unique creation. How does an employer treat a unique creation like you? They make you fit into a box where the walls are your job description. Many people before you had to fit into the same box and many people after you will have to do the same. You were not created to spend your life following orders, doing repetitive tasks and being just like other people. Your own business offers you the opportunity to make unique achievements, to build a unique business, which mirrors your personality, and to stamp the world with your mark.

iii) If you do not want to start a business to create personal wealth or to satisfy your ego then start a business to help other people. Every time a person offers others a new product or service, he or she increases their freedom of choice. There is not a better way to help other people than by giving them more freedom. With the extra freedom, the jobs created and extra taxes paid, it could be argued that founding a successful business is the most socially useful thing anyone can do. Instead of choosing between i), ii) or iii) as a reason for starting a business, all three become interlocked and are a consequence of a successful business.

Idea Generation:
Most people unfamiliar with starting a business struggle to generate business ideas and that's where this book (and its companion 247 More Inspirational Ideas to Start Your Own Home Business) comes in. The ideas it contains will help you to generate ideas for yourself. The 'Foolish Ideas' will help you to see that the most unlikely things have made their originators rich.
Also these people were no better educated, more intelligent or talented than you are. The only difference between these successful people and you is that they took action. Action is the key to success, without action, your idea will never be anything more than an electrical impulse locked away in your brain.

Action is the Key

Many people for one reason or another, find it difficult to take action. They procrastinate about doing the things they really want to do. Most importantly these are the things that will have a huge impact on their life and turn it around for the better. For sure, they are great at coming up with excuses, but excuses are about the only thing that they do generate.

If you talk to people who procrastinate, they often describe their condition like it is some genetic defect and that it is incurable, save a miracle. If you happen to fall into this category then I have some hard-hitting news for you. Procrastination is nothing more than a bad habit, like nail-biting, and for whatever reasons you are doing it, you are not doomed to a lifetime of procrastination. You can get over it. There are many effective techniques that have been designed to stop you putting things off, and more importantly they work. I have personally experienced the transformation of ex-procrastinators into hard-workers, simply from using these techniques below.

People who get things done, are also far happier than people who waste time agonising over doing things, but then don't do them. I would estimate that not doing something is easily five times more painful than actually doing it. And once you start, you will often find that you're enjoying yourself.

Procrastinators also lack energy. Brains are curious bits of our anatomy. Using them turns on a positive flow of energy which makes us feel good, and the longer we are absorbed in doing something, the better we feel. Stopping shuts down this flow of energy. Of course brains need a rest as well, but only for ten minutes every hour or two. Worrying about not doing something is exhausting, whereas absorbing yourself in a task is energizing and makes you feel good.

The hardest thing to overcome is getting started and there are several strategies that work. The first is to tell yourself you will only do the task for five minutes. Even the laziest sloth on the planet can usually motivate him or herself to tackle something for this length of time. This is rather sneaky, because once people have got over the pain of starting, they are quite willing to carry on.

It also helps to set yourself goals:

Write down how much you plan to do before a certain time. For example, "I will finish writing chapter 2 before lunch time, only when I have finished chapter 2 will I stop for lunch."

Also write down all the jobs that you need to do in order of importance and do them one by one. Only when you have completed the first task should you go on to the next. It is also better to do the worst job first, then once this is out of the way you will no longer have it hanging over you. This allows you to do the other jobs with an increased sense of relief and satisfaction.

Writing all your jobs down is a really powerful technique for zooming through everything that you need to do and you will get an amazing amount of gratification from ticking each item off. Try it for yourself. You'll be pleasantly surprised at how much more productive you become.

Part 1
30 'Foolish' Ideas Which Made Their Creator's Rich

Why am I starting out telling the stories of other people who have made it big? After all I'm supposed to be giving you ideas to use, not businesses that are already successful and 'used up'. For 2 reasons:

1. The biggest cause of people not getting into business in the first place (or getting out at the first sign of difficulty) is belief. You have to believe in yourself and in your idea. You have to believe that someone like you can be a success. Without belief you won't get started. These stories should inspire you to believe you can make things happen.

2. No line of business or niche is ever quite 'full'. You might feel, reading through the massive success of some of these entrepreneurs, that there's no room for you in the area of business they're in. Don't be fooled, there are often ways to do similar things better, faster, easier, or with a twist.

You'll discover a few key things from this section:

* Lack of education makes absolutely no difference, its NOT a stumbling block in any way to making millions.

* Environment and upbringing make no difference, creating no barriers at all to becoming rich.

* The harder you work, the more you earn is a TOTAL fallacy!

* Anyone - really - anyone can get rich, honestly and ethically.

The stories are necessarily brief, but the essential details are there. Some may be a little dated now, as they have been collected over a long period. But that shouldn't matter, the fact is these people all had an idea for a business and succeeded. I hope you will be inspired to dream up your own idea and to make as much money as you want to from it.

You can do it - these stories contain all the proof you need.

A 'Dumb' Pupil Makes a Fortune From Furniture!

Name: Terri Bowersock.
Nationality: American.
Age: At 22 opened her first store.
'Foolish' Idea: Selling second-hand furniture back to the general public.
Start-up Capital: Borrowed $2,000 from grandmother.
How Idea was Launched: Opened a store in Mesa, Arizona - Terri's Consign and Design Furnishings Store. Her mother's living room furniture and her own bedroom furniture was her entire stock in the shop.
Sales: Although it took 2 weeks to make her first sale, by the end of the second year, sales were $4,000 a month and rising. 10 years later she opened her second store. Now, there are seven stores in the Phoenix area, and also another six franchise stores.
Earnings: Terri's Consign and Design Furnishings now has 167 employees and annual revenues of $16million.

Terri Bowersock is dyslexic, but she refused to use that as an excuse to hinder her from making millions of dollars. Her fifth-grade teacher told her she was as dumb as a cue ball, but being dyslexic, doesn't mean she's stupid. Although she managed to graduate, her reading ability was third-grade level, which meant she was unable to fill-in a job application. So, she landed up doing poorly paid jobs. She washed windows and then sold sandwiches at a golf course. But eventually, she landed a job in a consignment shop, and figured; she could get other people's furniture, display it in a store and sell it.

Borrowing $2,000 from her grandmother, and displaying her mother's living room furniture and her own bedroom furniture, Terri opened her first shop. In 1997, Terri was named as one of Avon's Women of Enterprise. She has also been featured in an 'Outstanding Dyslexus' Calendar.

Terri gets other people to handle her contracts, because she can't read them, and also to balance her cheque book. She has two main beliefs: always be straight and honest with your customers - that way they return again and again, and don't let any handicap, problem or difficulty put you off. Terri hasn't allowed any obstacles to stand in her way and now she's a millionaire.

A £20,000 Loan into Millions - Thanks to Reggie Perrin!

Name: Jonathan Elvidge.
Nationality: British.
Age: 27 when opened The Gadget Shop in Hull, 1991.
'Foolish' Idea: A shop full of unusual gadgets. From inflatable aliens, to lava lamps and night-vision goggles.
Start-up Capital: Jonathan had made a lot of money by moving house in the late eighties. Re-mortgaging the new property gave him some capital but he needed a further £20,000. The bank loaned him the full £20,000 on the Government Scheme for Small Firms - the Government secured 70 per cent of the loan.
How Idea was Launched: Rented a unit in a new shopping centre in Hull.
Sales: Started with one shop in Hull. Formed partnership with Andrew Hobbs, who bought half the company. By, the end of the first year, they had 3 shops. To date, 31 outlets. Their best selling product is the lava lamp. They purchased them before their renewed popularity.
Earnings: Business empire is now worth over £50million.

When Jonathan Elvidge fell out with his employer at the telephone company in Hull where he worked, he decided to have a go at running his own business. His love for gadgets and watching the Fall and Rise of Reginald Perrrin, gave him the money-making idea he needed. The Grot shop in the series, and not being able to buy the type of gifts he wanted to, inspired the idea of a shop filled with unusual affordable gadgets. He researched products and how to get a unit, before approaching banks for a £20,000 loan; which he needed to top up his own financial reserves to open the first shop.

The day he opened his first shop, there was just himself, a friend and baby-sitter to serve customers. Because Jonathan had not realised all the other retailers in the shopping centre had negotiated the rent on their units, he had accepted the £30,000 a year rental charge without question. It left him only breaking even, despite working a 60 hour week. He wanted to open more shops, but was unable to raise the capital.

Andrew Hobbs, who was in charge of letting the shopping centre units, suggested a partnership. Jonathan agreed and before the end of the first year, they had opened two more shops. Jonathan spends most of his time travelling to trade fairs, especially in the Far East, to select products. Jonathan Elvidge went from working for a telephone company to owning a business partnership worth over £50million from his idea.

Helping Son with Maths Makes Mother $Millions!
Name: Judith Bliss.
Nationality: American.
Age: 48 yrs.
'Foolish' Idea: A computer game designed to help children learn maths. Judith's idea was to fuse an adventure story with math quizzes. She called the game, 'Math Magic'.
Start-up Capital: Unknown.
How Idea was Launched: Started own business - Mindplay. Sold Math Magic and went on to develop several more computer games.
Sales: Sells mostly to Schools - by mailing.
Earnings: Tuscon-based company, Mindplay earned $1.4 million in revenues in 1 yr.

Judith Bliss was born into a family who were 'dirt poor', as she says. Her dad was a compulsive gambler, who went to jail for writing bad cheques, when Judith was 11. Her mother had to take in laundry, and slave for 12 hours a day, just to make ends meet, barely. So, Judith grew up realising how important a good education is. She studied hard and after getting a degree in maths at College, she got a job as a computer programmer. She married and life was good until her marriage turned sour when David was only 4.

Judith continued to work hard and look after her son. But, her son was complaining he found school boring, while his teachers insisted that he just couldn't learn. However, Judith noticed her son, spent hours at his computer. It gave her an idea. What if she could create a programme, which combined adventures with solving mathematical equations? A computer game which made learning maths fun? So, she worked on a new programme, where the object is to get terribly cute little creatures out of mean Queen Grudgeon's dungeon, by multiplying and dividing a series of fractions. It's the only way to get the creatures out, otherwise they stay locked up forever!

It worked. Her son, David, loved the programme and after just 3 months his grades improved. This made Judith think if the game had helped her son, it would help other children. So, she started her own business, selling her game - which she called Maths Magic - by mailing to schools. David eventually became an honours student and his mother enjoys a six-figure income.

Losing a Race Powers a $100million-a-year Business!
Name: Brian Maxwell, Jennifer Biddulph (now Jennifer Maxwell).
Nationality: Canadian.
Ages: Not known.
'Foolish' Idea: A source of instant energy food which marathon runners and other athletes could eat, even while on the move. A nutritious, tasty, easily digested, energising food bar. The result: PowerBars.
Start-Up Capital: Unknown.

How Idea was Launched: In a tiny cellar space, Brian and Jennifer produced 40,000 PowerBars. They travelled to sporting events, sold the bars and gave out samples and discount coupons. Brian also approached Quaker Oats, but they weren't interested. The U.S. Cycling team offered sponsorship in exchange for free PowerBars. The resulting CBS broadcasting short story, gave them advertising coverage which launched the company into production.
Sales: Mainly to athletes and sports people.
Earnings: $100million-a-year business.

Four-time Canadian National Champion marathon runner, Brian Maxwell, suffered a heartbreaking setback, when stomach problems and running out of energy, nearly forced him out of a marathon. He was leading in front of 7,000 competitors while competing in the Manchester Marathon (England) - a grueling 26-mile race.

Despite falling apart physically and emotionally, Brian stayed with the race, coming in seventh, instead of winning. However, it made him think, if there had been a small convenient, easy to eat source of energy available, he could have overcome his dilemma during the race. But such a food, simply didn't exist. So Brian determined to produce his own food bar. He teamed up with UC Berkeley nutrition and food science student, Jennifer Biddulph, also a competitive runner. In Brian's kitchen, they mixed breakfast cereals, fruit juices, vitamin pills, and milk powder. The results were not encouraging. Each combination of mixture merely ended up as a horrible mess of 'glop'. They persevered and three years and 800 combinations later they worked out the winning formula for a high energising bar that was also tasty and had the right consistency.

Producing 400 bars themselves, they loaded them into a Ford Falcon and began selling PowerBars, and giving out samples and discount coupons at sporting events. Jennifer and Brian had proved the bars worked and could sell, so Brian approached Quaker Oats. They weren't interested, but the U.S. Cycling team came to their rescue. They offered sponsorship in return for free PowerBars. CBS broadcast a short story and Jennifer and Brian were on their way to winning with a $100million-a-year business.

Water Turns Into Liquid Riches!

Name: Debora Mache (Co-owner). Owner: unknown.
Nationality: American.
Age: Unknown.
'Foolish' Idea: A bar where the only drink served is bottled water from all corners of the world.
Start-Up Capital: Cost of opening a bar. Amount: not known.
How Idea was Launched: Opened a water bar in Boston.
Sales: The Waterbar in Boston is doing so well, that Debora is considering opening another one in San Francisco.
Earnings: Not known (project is new).

Alcohol-free drinking at the Waterbar on Boston's hip South End is enjoyed by a cross-section of mainly young business people. The drinks served range from water at 75 cents a small bottle, like Poland Spring, to more exotic waters of Italy or Fiji for $4 or $5 each. There are also caffeine-containing waters like 'Krank 20'.

Debra believes that The Waterbar is a success, because water is the most pure, simple substance to drink. The interior design of The Waterbar is clean cut and modern, using several shades of blue for the walls, and silver grey for an upbeat look. Rows of bottled water neatly stacked, line the wall behind the silver coloured bar.

Appreciation of the attention to detail of the surroundings is borne out by the customers. Salesman, John Ranco, 36, says The Waterbar is a nice escape and environment. Although this is a new venture, the Boston Waterbar is doing so well, that Debora Mache is considering opening another one in San Francisco. She could well be on her way to striking it rich from simply selling water.

Unemployed Mother to £50million Top Author!

Name: Joanne Rowling.
Nationality: British.
Age: 34yrs
'Foolish' Idea: A skinny boy wearing large glasses, called Harry Potter. The character is an orphan who escapes to Hogswarts School of Witchcraft and Wizadry, and becomes a hero.
Start-up Capital: A few pounds.
How Idea was Launched: Through an agent. Two publishing houses rejected the book, before Bloomsbury accepted in 1996.
Sales: Worldwide. 1 book - Harry Potter and the Philosopher's Stone. More than 38 weeks as No.1 on the New York Times bestseller list. 2nd book - Harry Potter and the Chamber of Secrets. 3rd book - Harry Potter and the Prisoner of Azkaban. 30 Million books sold. America accounts for approximately 50 per cent of the sales. Translated into 28 languages.
Earnings: Royalties of around £11.5million in addition to advance payments of £2million for the second and third books. Now the 3rd, 4th and 5th books plus the phenomenally successful film make the likely earnings far higher, possibly approaching £50 million eventually.
Spin-offs: Film rights to the first book, Harry Potter and the Philosopher's Stone. Lightning-bolt 'tattoos' to stick onto the forehead (Harry Potter has identical scar).
Earnings from Spin-offs: £1million for the film rights. Tattoos - unknown.

Divorced single mum, Joanne Rowling, was desperate to escape the freezing cold one-bedroom apartment in Edinburgh, where she was bringing up her daughter Jessica. In search of warmth, Joanne would go to the nearest café and order one cup of coffee, which had to last for hours because she was so broke. Her plight gave her the courage to follow through the idea of writing a mystical cliffhanger novel. 29 yrs old and on state benefit, she thought the worst thing that could happen, would be if she was turned down by every publisher in the country. That inspired her to write, every day. In the mornings, Joanne would take Jessica to the park and walk around with her in the pushchair until she fell asleep, then she would head to the nearest café, and write for up to two hours while her daughter slept.

Once again in the evenings, as soon as Jessica was in bed, Joanne would write until she dropped. Although writing Harry Potter and the Philosopher's Stone was hard work it kept her sane. When the book was written, Joanne had another problem; she couldn't afford to buy a computer to type the manuscript. So, instead, she paid a few pounds for an old battered typewriter and typed it out. Next Joanne had to type out another copy, because she couldn't afford the photocopying costs.

She used the telephone directory to pick out two agents and posted the book to each one. She says it was her happiest moment when one of them agreed to represent her. The first book was published in Britain, June 1997. Harry Potter was a huge success quickly achieving soaring sales and popularity. Joanne admits the whole venture has gone beyond her wildest expectations. Although the Potter series are children's fantasy adventure stories they have also captivated an adult following. Just as J.R.R. Tolkien's, Lord of the Rings. The books are also being likened to such earlier classics as The Wizard of Oz, Alice in Wonderland and The Narnia Chronicles. The magic of Harry Potter, in a fantasy world of witchcraft and wizardry looks set to becoming another classic hero. A character who has, through just 3 adventures, made its creator £50million.

Smash-hit TV Game Makes Trio Millionaires!

Names: David Briggs, Mike Whitehill, Steve Knight.
Nationalities: British.
Ages: David, 49. Mike, 39 and Steve, 29.

'Foolish' Idea: A television quiz show, 'Who Wants To Be a Millionaire?', where audiences at home, watch real people make decisions which could affect their lives.
Start-Up Capital: Zero.
How Idea was Launched: The show was produced by the television production company, Celador.
Sales: The English programme is hosted by Chris Tarrant. The American version, features Regis Philbin. 'Who Wants To Be a Millionaire?' is shown in 40 countries.
Earnings: Millions of pounds over the years in royalties. Specified amount of earnings to date, not known.
Spin-offs: A board game and computer game of the hit TV show.
Earnings from Spin-offs: Unknown.

David Briggs, wrote down an idea for a TV show on a scrap of paper. He wanted to come up with a formula, which had the audiences on the edge of their seats as they watched contestants make decisions which could affect their lives. The final idea, had even more audience participation. 'Who Wants To Be a Millionaire?' studio audiences can directly affect a contestant's level of winnings by answering a question for a contestant who doesn't know the answer.

The winning formula of the smash-hit TV show, watched in 40 countries, and by millions of people in Britain alone, was created by trio, Steve Knight, David Briggs and Mike Whitehill, who have spent years coming up with TV game show ideas. They originally met when the three worked together at a radio station in London. The show has exceeded all expectations and left even the trio amazed at the worldwide success.

The creators believe that a secret of the show's success is that each contestant in the hot seat facing Chris Tarrant, is there, because they answered questions correctly and not because they are beautiful or friends with someone in television. Anyone watching at home, also know they could be a contestant, and that the people on the show are just like them. Contestants have the real chance to win one million pounds by answering general knowledge questions.

It's a TV game with high audience participation and a game which has made the trio who created it, winners and future millionaires.

Postman's Game Gives Him a Sporting Chance to Get Rich!

Name: Robert Poole.
Nationality: American.
Age: Not known.
'Foolish' Idea: A board game about sports rules, called, 'Rules of the Game'.
Start-up Capital: He collected $530,000 from the residents of his town, where he delivers the post.
How Idea was Launched: Robert Poole wanted to produce and market the game himself. So he set up a company for people to buy stock which gave him the finance. 300 people put in a total of $530,000. Robert designed the prototype. Next, the game was laid out on the computer. 'Rules of the Game' had to be printed, and trademarks had to be paid for. Robert set up an 800 free-phone number and began selling the game through a network of small merchants. Then Kmart got interested and the game took off.
Sales: Kmart sold 20,000 boxes of the board game over the Christmas period, in a trial run in 900 of their stores. It's now being sold in 2,100 of their stores all over the U.S.
Earnings: The game retails at $29.95. Earnings unknown.

Coaching youngsters in baseball during his free time, gave Postman, Robert Poole, an idea for a board game. Living in the small town of Clayton, North Carolina, with a population of 8,000, he was friends with most of the people on his mail delivery route.

Knowing he coached baseball, he would be asked about incidents that had occurred in their kid's games. Robert would try to answer their questions. Then it became a game with his workmates, which made Robert decide to invent a game about sports rules for all the sports fans out there.

Mary, his mother, helped him design a prototype in 1993. Robert came up with 580 questions, divided into 4 sports - baseball, basketball, football and golf. The players roll a dice, then answer questions, like they do in Trivial Pursuit. But it looked as though the project would go no further, because he couldn't raise the money to produce and market the game, on his $36,000 a year salary. He also had a wife and two boys, Ryan 7 and Corey, 3, to consider.

Along his delivery route, Robert began telling his 300 customers about the game he'd designed. Amazingly, they thought it was such a good idea, they wanted to back him. They bought stock in a company Robert set up, in amounts ranging from $1,000 to $50,000.

After selling Rules of the Game, through a network of small merchants, through an 800 freephone number, Kmart became interested. A Christmas try-out in 900 of their stores, resulted in sales of 20,000. Robert is still building his business.

Homemade Nail Polish makes Sisters Rich!

Names: Anna and Sarah Levinson.
Nationality: American.
Ages: Anna, 20. Sarah, 18.
'Foolish' Idea: The sisters enjoy wearing nail varnish, but couldn't find the colours they wanted. After mixing their own shades of varnish, friends and classmates liked the colours so much, the sisters realised they had a good business idea.
Start-up Capital: Cash from $27,000 of stock - which they'd been given at birth - was added to a loan from their grandmother (loan amount not known).

How Idea was Launched: In 1995, they started the company, RIPE. A small boutique ordered the vibrant pastel shades. Next, a larger store ordered 100 bottles. Anna and Sarah mixed and made the nail polish themselves, they also filled bottles purchased from a local beauty supply store and used hand-made labels. Macy's ordered thousands of bottles of RIPE nail varnish.
Sales: Each bottle sells for $7. Just one year in business and the sisters had sold more than $150,000 worth of product.
Earnings: The business soon topped over $1million-a-year.

Sisters Anna and Sarah, from Los Angeles, began their business while still at school. They both loved wearing unusual colour nail varnish, and invariably ended up mixing their own shades, because the shops simply didn't stock what they wanted. Friends, classmates and even shopkeepers, asked the girls where they bought their nail varnish. So, they decided to cash in stocks worth, $27,000 which they'd been given at birth, and start-up their own company, producing bottles of nail varnish in the colours they were always mixing up for themselves. Their grandmother gave them a loan, to top up their funds and RIPE was officially born.

Today, Macy's and other top stores stock their product. The girls have come up with over 60 shades of polish, retailing at $7 a bottle. The polishes carry exotic names - emerald forest, raisin, buttercup, shark and meteor, are just a handful. Their customers range from young trendsetting girls to funky grandmas. Celebrities also like to use RIPE. Tori Spelling wears cumulus and Demi Moore's favourite shade is kelp. Now a line of lipsticks have also been introduced. Anna and Sarah have turned painting their nails, into a $million business.

Worldwide Web Makes Penniless Islanders Rich!
Name: Islanders of South Pacific Nation of Tuvalu.
Nationality: Polynesian.
'Foolish' Idea: Selling their Internet address, which ends in 'TV'.

Start-up Capital: Zero - marketing company approached the islanders with offer.
How Idea was Launched: A company that markets Internet addresses, signed a deal with Tuvalu to sell its Internet address to buyers worldwide.
Sales: The company sells address to TV stations and other businesses in the television industry.
Earnings: An up-front fee of $50 million was paid by the marketer. For each of the 9,000 citizens in Tuvalu that's $5,500. The islanders also expect to earn a total of $300million in commissions over the next 10 years.

The 9,000 citizens of a Polynesian nation, living on the 16-square mile island of Tuvalu, live in simple thatch huts and eat a diet of fish and coconuts. But their lives have been changed forever - by the Internet. For this small island, located 650 miles north of the Fiji islands, is already planning to build schools, hospitals, houses and roads with the $300million they'll receive from commissions for selling their Internet address, which ends in TV.

Stranger than fiction; although the Internet is directly responsible for catapulting this society from living in a simple primitive manner to the comforts of modern living - the islanders can't surf the web themselves, because the country isn't yet connected to the Internet.

Collection of Celebrities' Hair Locks Worth a Cool $1million!

Name: John Reznikoff.
Age: Not known.
'Foolish' Idea: Many people treasure a lock of hair from a loved one. John decided to collect hair from famous people of the past.
Start-up Capital: Unknown.
How Idea was Launched: John travels the globe to track down locks. Owns, 'University Archives Inc.' of Stamford, Connecticut.

Sales: His collection includes locks, from dead celebrities: Abraham Lincoln, Marilyn Monroe and John F. Kennedy.
Earnings: Note: Research has not revealed if John Raznikoff's collection is for sale or on show to spectators. However, it has been included, because it's such an unusual idea for making money.

John Reznikoff has spent the past five years, travelling the world, tracking down locks of hair from 100s of different heads - all dead celebrities.

A celebrity memorabilia shop in Chevy Chase, Md., Norma Jean's, sells locks of hair at hair-raising prices. Strands of George Washington's hair for $1,600. Hair clipped the night Abraham Lincoln was shot, so doctors could tend his fatal head wound for $3,500. The famous locks of Elvis Presley that had to be cut at the start of his military career, clippings for $1,995. A John F Kennedy portrait with sealed plastic sleeve containing his hair, cut by barber Henry Gelbert for $2,200. No wonder John Reznikoff has his hair-raising collection insured for $1million.

$78million-a-year Selling Old Clothes!

Name: Vahan Chamlian.
Nationality: Armenian. Immigrant - America (40 years ago).
Age: 66 yrs.
'Foolish' Idea: In some countries, American clothes are considered a status symbol. Vahan realised if he purchased unwanted garments at rock bottom prices from Charity shops, he could afford to sell them in other countries.
Start-up Capital: Arrived in America 40 years ago with $20 in his pocket.
How Idea was launched: Visited charity shop dealers like the Salvation Army and Goodwill. Bought unwanted garments.
Sales: Sold to any country where American clothes are desired as a status symbol. Today owns more than a dozen business enterprises, employing over 800 people.

Earnings: His Los Angeles-based companies, last year, earned $78 million.

Not all the garments donated to charities are sold, because even people who visit charity shops are discerning shoppers, and don't want some of the donated clothes on offer. Immigrant, Vahan Chamlian, knew that in some countries, American clothes are considered a status symbol. So he turned buying rags into riches.

Bernie Brill, president of Secondary Materials and Recyclable Textiles, a Bethesda, Md., trade association, says that if it wasn't for people like Vahan, a lot of the clothes from charity shops would end up in landfills. Vahan turns garbage into gold, and gives extra funds to charities by buying unwanted garments. Armenia-born Vahan Chamlian, landed on American soil 40 years ago with just $20 in his pocket. Now, 66, he owns a million-dollar mansion, a private jet and a cadillac with personalised plate, 'LA RAGS.'

His donations to charity have funded many worthy causes, and he paid for a private elementary school to be built, donating it to Glendale, California. The Armenia Fund, recently received $500,000 from Vahan and his wife Anoush.

All this - and $78million-a-year business empire - just from selling unwanted clothes.

Sewing Bedsheet Corners Brought Housewife a $1million Plus Deal!

Name: Giselle Jubinville.
Nationality: Canadian.
Age: 41 yrs.
'Foolish' Idea: A fitted bottom bed sheet, that stayed put instead of popping off the mattress.
Start-up Capital: Nearly $16,000 - borrowed from friends and family - for the patent.

How Idea was launched: Secured the patent from office in Washington, D.C. The two largest Canadian sheet manufacturers were not interested in her design. So, she tried Springs Industries in the U.S., and they purchased her patent.
Sales: Through Springs Industries.
Earnings: Giselle was paid $1million plus for the sale of the patent.

Housewife Giselle Jubinville, can hardly sew a stitch, but she was so fed-up with fitted sheets that kept popping off mattress corners that she decided to design a better fitted sheet - one that really did stay put.

For two months, day and night, she tried hundreds of designs, using just her old sewing machine. Everyone told her she was crazy and even experts said she was wasting her time, because you can't patent a sheet. But, Giselle was determined and wouldn't give up, even sewing in the corner of her bedroom all night, while her husband, Leonard, slept.

The breakthrough came, when one night she saw the perfect design in a dream. By stitching the corners at just the right angle and using slightly more fabric, she was able to make a deeper pocket, and the sheet remained in place, because the pocket stayed on any mattress.

Despite designing the perfect fitted sheet, it took Giselle of St. Albert, Alberta, Canada, another 4 years to sell her design. The patent office in Washington, D.C. turned her down three times, because there were already more than 100 patented ways of sewing sheet corners, so they didn't agree that Giselle's idea was new. Furious, she travelled to Washington, taking with her a miniature mattress and the new sheet corner. Once the patent examiner had been shown the design he agreed it was new, and awarded a patent.

Next stop was the two largest Canadian sheet manufacturers. However, Giselle suffered a devastating setback when both companies were not in the least bit interested in purchasing her design. But when she tried Springs Industries in the U.S., they purchased her patent for a $1million plus. Now Giselle and her family are enjoying the results of her 'foolish' idea - a four-bedroom dream house newly built, they are on easy street and having a ball.

Hi-Tec Trash Earns Piles of Cash!

Names: Davis and Betsy Gilbert.
Ages: Unknown.
'Foolish' Idea: Davis and Betsey got their moneymaking idea after discovering that gold is used in circuits and other computer parts. Their company, Electronic Recovery Specialists, extracts the gold and other precious metals from old computers.
Start-up Capital: Undisclosed.
How Idea was Launched: They bought old equipment from hospitals, universities and corporations, then scraped dust-sized amounts of gold. Started up their own company, Electronic Recovery Specialists.
Sales: The recycled gold is used by everyone from jewellers to dentists.
Earnings: More than $7million a year.

Every week, industry discards tons of old computers and little of it is recycled. That is, not until Davis and Betsy Gilbert hit upon the idea to extract the gold and other precious metals for recycling. But it's not just computers that contain precious metals, they are also to be found in telephones, satellites, mobile phones, connectors and phone equipment.

Their Chicago company, Electronic Recovery Specialists, goes through tons of old computers every week, taking them apart and extracting precious metals from the circuit boards. At first, it was tedious work, taking hours to scrape dust-sized amounts of gold from the tiny pins in circuit boards. Now Davis has engineered a quick method that allows his company to extract from 10 tons of computers a week. Davis's method remains his secret. Extracting precious metals for recycling, from old, hi-tec office equipment, has created a company that the couple estimate will make more than $7 million this year.

The Balzac Balloon Ball Tops Sales of $100million!

Name: Mary Rodas.
Nationality: American.
Age: 14 yrs.
'Foolish' Idea: A wild coloured and patterned ball created by blowing up a balloon inside a sturdy cloth sack.
Start-up Capital: Not known.
How Idea was Launched: By the New York City toy company, Catco, Inc.
Sales: Toy shops
Earnings: The Balzac Balloon Ball sales have topped $100 million. Mary was hired as vice president of marketing, for Catco, Inc. at a salary of $200,000 a year.

Mary Rodas started in the toy business, at the tender age of just 4 yrs. Her dad worked as a janitor at a New Jersey apartment building where the toy executive, Donald Spector, lived. Over the years Donald gave Mary new products to test. She proved to be an amazing judge of what kids like, her opinions always right on target. At 14, Mary was helping Donald Spector to pick out so many winners that he hired her as vice president of marketing, on a salary of $200,000 a year.

Mary scored an instant success with the 'Balzac', a ball made by blowing up a balloon inside a sturdy cloth sack. When Mary suggested wild colours and patterns should go on the sack, sales shot through the roof - topping $100million. Mary Rodas, at the tender age of 14, was earning $200,000 a year.

'Auntie Anne's Pretzels Rise to $80million-a-year!

Name: Ann Beiler.
Nationality: American.
Age: 48 yrs.
'Foolish' Idea: Cooking pretzels with different ingredients to her competitors.
Start-up Capital: $6,000.
How Idea was Launched: Ann purchased a farmer's market booth.
Sales: Started in 1988. After perfecting her pretzels, sales were $1,500 a weekend. By 1989, Ann had opened 8 stores throughout Pennsylvania, including her first mall location. Next, she franchised the concept. There are now over 400 Auntie Anne's pretzel stores across America and in several other countries.
Earnings: $80million-a-year empire.

The turning point in Ann Beiler's meteoric rise in business was the result of a mistake, which eventually led to an empire of over 400 stores. The 48 year old, mother of two, took a low-paid job, managing a pizza and pretzel booth at a farmer's market, to financially help her husband's new counselling service. Another farmer's market booth came up for sale at $6,000 and Ann decided to buy it. She borrowed the money from a family member.

At first, her sales were just steady, but that all changed when a supplier delivered the wrong ingredients. Ann had to make up her pretzels with different ingredients and sales quadrupled to $1,500 a weekend. Her ingredient mixtures are still a trade secret, known only to the franchisees.

Auntie Anne's was ranked as the top franchise in the pretzel industry by the Entrepreneur magazine in 1996. Today, Auntie Annie's produce freshly baked pretzels in cinnamon sugar, sour cream and onion, whole wheat, garlic, sesame, caramel almond and raisin flavours. The pretzels sell for less than $2, and Auntie Anne guarantees her pretzels will never be out of the oven more than 30 minutes. Ann Beiler believes her secret to success is making a difference in business by giving of yourself. Today, Ann donates $100,000 a year to the counselling service her husband started and built an $80million-a-year empire - all from a mistake which led her to the simple idea of cooking her pretzels with different ingredients.

Face-lifting Old Industrial Buildings Builds Profits of £4million!

Names: Tom Bloxham and Jonathan Falkingham.
Nationality: Both British.
Ages: Tom, 35. Jonathan - not known.
'Foolish' Idea: To convert unwanted buildings into smart housing.
Start-up Capital: Not known.
How Idea was Launched: They started the Urban Splash property company. The 1st building they purchased was a chemical lab.
Sales: Housing for domestic use.
Earnings: Urban Splash made a profit of £4million last year and has £100million worth of projects on the go.

Tom Bloxham and Architect Jonathan Falkingham set up the Urban Splash property company in 1993, buying old inner-city industrial buildings which are often in a decaying or dilapidated state. They pioneered developing these unwanted buildings into tasteful, often upmarket apartments, in the North-west. There is usually a queue of buyers, ready to move into the smart apartments built by the company. Tom spends most of his time searching out buildings suitable for development and finding good people to manage the conversions. Tom and Jonathan now employ nearly 300 people.

Their first project was a chemical lab, which had great windows and exposed brickwork. Tom, says he wants to make Urban Splash the designer brand of housing.

Tom's own 'success' tips: You need a strong idea and the determination to succeed with it. It's important to treat people, in the same way you'd like to be treated. Don't be afraid to ask for what you want, and go straight to the people at the top of an organisation.

Urban Splash is certainly a successful company with £100million worth of projects in hand and a profit of £4million made last year.

Converting a Car Part, makes Hair Stylist a Multimillionaire!

Name: Denie Schach.
Nationality: American.
Age: 45 yrs.
'Foolish' Idea: An easy way to create fashionable upswept hairstyles, such as the French Twist.
Start-up-Capital: $1,000.
How Idea was Launched: Denie showed her invention to Bradley Business Builders which is a company that specialises in helping entrepreneurs launch their ideas on the market place. Started her own Dallas based company, Angelhair.
Sales: The first shipment of 30,000 'Hairdinis' sold out. They're sold to hairdressers, salons, mall boutiques and major department stores.
Earnings: Over $20million in sales. Denie is a multimillionaire.

Denie Schach went from a struggling hairdresser who spent sleepless nights worrying about how the family could pay the bills, to becoming a multimillionaire. When clients began asking her if she knew of an easier way to create upswept hairstyles, Denie began to experiment with using a bendable foam covered wire as support for the styles.

Fifteen different prototypes all proved unsuccessful, and at one stage she was so discouraged that she threw a prototype into the dustbin. Then she tried the sturdy durable foam used on the inner roof of cars, and it worked perfectly.

Denie took her finished invention to specialists in bringing new ideas to market, Bradley Business Builders. Both Denie and her husband, John, had to put their own money into the project as well, but the gamble paid off. The first shipment of 30,000 Hairdinis sold out. Now, Denie sells the $30 Hairdini, complete with an instructional video and how-to-booklets, directly to the public by appearing regularly on QVC. It's also purchased by hairdressing salons, boutiques and major department stores.

Dennie's advice to other people with an idea: If you believe in the idea, don't give up on it, no matter how silly other people think it is. Don't take no for an answer. Your wildest dreams can become a reality.

A simple hair styling product has made Denie a multimillionaire.

Selling Mobiles from a Flat to £millions Profits!

Name: Charles Dunstone.
Nationality: British.
Age: 24 when began business.
'Foolish' Idea: Spotted potential for mobile phones in the consumer marketplace.
Start-up Capital: Savings of £6,000.
How Idea was Launched: Put an ad in the Evening Standard. Did business over the phone at first, working from a flat on London's Marylebone Road.
Sales: Opened first shop for Carphone Warehouse, within a year. There are now over 180 branches in the UK and 160 overseas.
Earnings: Charles has a half share of the company profits which last year were about £20million.

Charles Dunstone worked for the Japanese electronics company, NEC. When he got transferred to their mobile phone division as a sales manager, he began to see the potential of selling mobiles to the consumer market place.

He left NEC, and using £6,000 of savings, he hired three staff and started up Carphone Warehouse.

From an advert he placed in the Evening Standard, orders came in by phone. He knew a few people in the business who could supply him and within the first year, Charles and his three staff moved from working at a flat in Marylebone Road to opening the first Carphone Warehouse Shop.

Charles's target was to be known as an honest broker who recommended the best and most cost-effective mobile for people's needs. That dedication paid off when they won a concession to sell mobile phones in Harrods. Although the profits were not high, it gave the company credibility. Every day Charles, gets up early to review the pricing of all their competitors, in order to stay one step ahead.

He puts the success down to: Giving top quality service, good value offers, good ads, location of shops and coming up with exciting new ideas to impress customers. Charles spends a lot of his time with people in networks and supplies negotiating good deals for his customers.

Selling mobiles has paid off for Charles Dunstone, company profits last year were about £20million, of which he has a half share.

Dyson Dual Cyclone Cleans Up a Fortune for Inventor!
Name: James Dyson.
Nationality: British.
Age: 53 yrs.

'Foolish' Idea: A vacuum cleaner without a dust bag that wouldn't clog and push the dirt around, instead of picking it up.
Start-up Capital: Retaining the patent, James raised money for research and production by selling licences in Japan.
How Idea was Launched: The Dyson Dual Cyclone was launched in 1993. James started his own company, Dyson, which has become one of the fastest growing manufacturing companies in the country.
Sales: First sold in Japan as the 'G Force', produced in pastel pink, it became a luxury status symbol, selling at £1,200 per machine. Currently making sales of £12million a year in Japan. Sales are made through all major stores.
Earnings: The company, Dyson, turns over £100million.

James Dyson is a former art student who didn't know a ball-bearing from a ballpoint pen, but still set out to invent a vacuum that would revolutionise cleaning our homes. Not a qualified engineer, James didn't even have an O level in physics. Yet, he invented the first vacuum cleaner which discarded the bag and replaced it with a little typhoon that spun at the speed of sound, in a chamber that couldn't clog.

James is a keen enthusiast on the importance of a good looking product with an intangible style, which sets that product apart. The Dual Cyclone is uniquely on permanent display at both the Science Museum and the Design Museum, and in the Twentieth Century Gallery at the V & A.

James's personal success steps: Observing objects in daily use, which it was always assumed could not be improved. Using lateral thinking, it is possible to arrive at an advance. There's no need to worry about not being an expert - after the idea there's plenty of time to learn the technology.

The first cyclonic vacuum cleaner James built, was out of cereal packets and masking tape, long before he understood how it worked. Retaining the patent, he tried to raise money for research and then production, by selling licences to America and Japan. The Japanese market was a success, with the machine being sold as the 'G Force' and produced in pastel pink, it became a luxury status symbol selling at £1,200 per machine.

America was not a success, because after a licence agreement was terminated, a gargantuan manufacturer began production and marketing a cyclonic vacuum cleaner under its own name. James took out a lawsuit and fought against the company for five years.

James Dyson took his idea, from a cereal box and masking tape, to the instantly recognisable, stylish Dyson Dual Cyclone cleaner. Now, James heads his company, Dyson, which is turning over £100 million.

Extra note: James Dyson has written a book of his personal story behind the invention, the Dyson Dual Cyclone which I recommend you rush out to buy and read. Title: Against the Odds.

Creating Clay Critters Rakes in the Dough - $13million!

Name: Kathleen Kelly.
Nationality: American.
Age: 48 yrs.
'Foolish' Idea: Collectible figurines and dolls made of clay.
Start-up Capital: Not known.
How Idea was Launched: Made figurines at home and sold them at craft fairs. Then a few stores bought her work. In 1985 Kathleen discovered a latex material she could use to make reproductions of her figurines so she started manufacturing them in her garage. She called the business, the Critter Factory.
Sales: 1st year's sales hit $50,000. By the 3rd year, the Critter Factory was a $300,000-a-year business. In 1990, she lost heart in the business and it went downhill. 3 months later, Russ Berrie and Co. paid her to license and reproduce her critters. They sell them around the world.

Earnings: A $25,000 advance royalty cheque for Kathleen, followed by further royalties. More than $13 million a year from sales.

Kathleen Kelly reckons she's the luckiest person in the universe. From her sprawling two and a half acre ranch home, in California, she creates clay critters. The wide range of collectible dolls and figurines are sold around the world, with sales ringing to the tune of $13 million a year.

But her journey was a long and often bumpy one. As a child, she'd make little accessories for her toys, like clay cows and fences. She earned an A in a college ceramics class, although she didn't finish college. At one of theses classes, when Kathleen went to retrieve pieces of her work from the kiln, she discovered her pottery had been stolen. She was thrilled that somebody liked her work that much, and the incident served to give her encouragement.

Eventually, Kathleen and her sister went into business together, selling pottery, mugs, plants and macrame hangers. In 1976 Kathleen had a daughter, Rachel, so she tried 'real' jobs, but the income wasn't enough to pay for child care. So she began making clay figurines at home, taking them to craft fairs. Several stores bought her work, but it was slow and painstaking making up each individual character.

In 1985, Kathleen married, and also discovered a latex material which revolutionised her work. Able to make true reproductions of her figurines, she manufactured them in the garage. The Critter Factory was born. The 1st years sales hit $50,000. In the 3rd year, the business grossed an annual figure of $300,000. However, in 1990, disaster struck. Kathleen divorced and the Critter Factory went downhill. Kathleen also now had two daughters to provide for, Rachel from before the marriage, and Christy, now 12, from her ex-husband.

The breakthrough came when a man who had phoned Kathleen several times before, offering to find licensing for her work, rang again. This time she gave him permission to go ahead. Three months later, Russ Berrie and Co., paid her $25,000 in advance royalty fees to license and reproduce her critters. Now, Kathleen and her two daughters are on easy street - thanks to a collection of collectible critters.

Organising Posh Parties nets £5million!

Name: Justin Etzin.
Nationality: British.
Age: 23 yrs.
'Foolish' Idea: Throwing posh parties for other people.
Start-up Capital: £1,800.
How Idea was Launched: When Justin organised his own party, it was more of a hobby. He threw an end of GCSEs bash at a London nightclub, while still at public school, Bedales. Named his posh party business, Capital VIP Events.
Sales: His clients are all high profile and include, Qantas, Gucci, Planet Hollywood and Coca-Cola.
Earnings: Justin says he is worth about £5 million.

23 year old Justin Etzin, is the son of one of the founders of the Brother electronics firm. However, his interests are not in electronics but the leisure and property industry.

While still at the public school, Bedales, he threw a bash at a London night club and started his posh-party idea, calling it, Capital VIP Events. For the first party he organised - which was at the time more of a hobby - he needed 300 people paying £6 a head to cover costs. He called everyone he knew, telling them it was going to be a brilliant party. They in turn, spread the word to their friends and 900 people ended up going to the party.

For his second party, he hired Ministry of Sound and Prodigy, at the time not knowing how he would pay for them. But, he said, failure was not an option, he merely looked at the goal and headed towards it. The event was such a success that he was not only able to pay the bands, but he was left with a profit.

Many of his clients are corporate companies and Prince William has attended one of the parties. For the launch of a new Gucci watch in 1996, Capital VIP Events hired famous models as waitresses. The guests could admire the watches worn by the models, round their necks and arms. Qantas asked for the Great Barrier Reef to be recreated for an event.

Account managers are in charge of each event. But, Justin oversees every part himself, from start to finish, often out all night - ready to walk (or crawl) into the office at 8.30 am. Partying is Justin's way of adding to his £5million fortune.

'Miss Attitude' Fashions Reuben into a Multi-Millionaire!
Name: Reuben Singh.
Nationality: British.
Age: 22 yrs.
'Foolish' Idea: To put all the cheaper fashion accessories together into a single store. For example: earrings and lipstick.
Start-up Capital: £4,000 savings.
How Idea was Launched: Reuben started selling female fashion accessories from a shopping centre kiosk in Manchester, using £4,000 he'd saved. He soon had the idea of taking all the cheaper items and selling them from a shop. He went round the local schools telling everyone he was opening a shop. He got 6,000 people along.
Sales: 'Miss Attitude', is now a chain of fashion accessory shops.
Earnings: Reuben sold the chain of shops and was entered into the 1998 Guinness Book of Records as Britain's youngest self-made millionaire, with an estimated wealth of £27.5 million.

At 22, the Reuben Singh Group of Companies stands at the capital value of £50 million. Reuben's now involved in currency trading, property, audio visual equipment and venture capital, but the greater part of his wealth to date, is from his first venture, the Miss Attitude chain of fashion accessory shops.

Using £4,000 he'd saved, Reuben began selling ladies fashion accessories in a shopping centre kiosk in Manchester, Rueben soon saw there was a market of putting all the cheap items, like earrings and lipsticks, into one shop.

But when he tried to rent a store in the shopping centre, the manager wouldn't take him seriously. Reuben discovered, he needed a retail agent, so he rang up the biggest in London. After some advice and leads, Reuben presented his idea again and this time the shopping centre management gave him 2 months to prove himself.

He visited all the local schools, telling pupils about his new shop and finally got 6,000 people along. Reuben went on to opening a chain of Miss Attitude shops and then sold the fashion empire.

Reuben has two Rolls-Royces, two Mercedes, two Ferraris a Porsche and a sports Bentley. But, although he loves boys' toys, the excitement for him is striving to go one better all the time. Most of his estimated wealth of £27.5million comes from his idea of selling all the cheap fashion accessories in one shop.

From $700 Business in a Basement to $30million-a-year!
Name: Kay Fredericks.
Nationality: American.
Age: 54 yrs.
'Foolish' Idea: Large, brightly coloured figures, illustrating educational subjects for pre-school aged children. The figures to be

interesting and full of texture, using yarn for hair and buttons for eyes.

Start-up Capital: $700 savings

How Idea was Launched: Kay's then husband, set up shop in a relative's basement and Trend Enterprises Inc., now with its head office in New Brighton, Minn., was born.

Sales: Products are sold in retail stores and catalogues. The firm, started in 1968, employs 175 people and markets 1,600 products in 43 countries.

Earnings: Trend Enterprises now generates over $30 million worth of sales a year.

It was while teaching at kindergarten that Kay Fredericks, first began developing her products, which eventually spawned her company, Trend Enterprises Inc.

Back in 1968, teachers of very young children had no educational aids, they had to produce their own. Kay had a massive bulletin board, and she made large, colourful childsize figures that the youngsters could relate to. To make the figures interesting she used yarn for hair and buttons for eyes. Teachers from all over the district were asking Kay to make figures for them.

But Kay never thought about giving up teaching until she had a car accident. Laying in hospital she had plenty of time to think, and decided that making learning items for other teachers was a sound business idea. She started with no business experience and just $700 savings. Her then husband set up a shop in a relative's basement. Over the years, the business went from a basement to a $30million-a-year corporation.

On the way, Kay had to build her credibility as a business woman. Financing was difficult and some male suppliers refused to deal with a woman. When one supplier asked the receptionist to get a man to help him, Kay, sent him packing.

Trend Enterprises Inc. produce everything from colourful flash cards to high-quality bulletin boards, and the company has a mission of educating children throughout the world. From kindergarten teacher to corporate leader, Kay turned $700 savings into a $30million a year empire that sells 1,600 products in 43 countries.

BodyLines Turn Curves into $12 million in 2 years!

Name: Julie Sautter.
Nationality: American.
Age: Unknown.
'Foolish' idea: A silicone pad made to wear outside the body, to give women cleavage without plastic surgery.
Start-up Capital: $100,000 borrowed money
How Idea was Launched: Set up shop in her garage. Julie asked a pal for technical advice on designing the product. Julie launched her product, Curves in 1994 and started up the company, BodyLines.
Sales: More than 250,000 women wear Curves, which are sold mainly through mail order and on TV. They are popular with actresses and TV designers.
Earnings: A TV station once sold $18,000 worth of Curves each minute. Within 2 years, the gross sales topped $12million. Expect $20million in sales for 3rd year in business.

After giving birth to her first child, Julie Sautter's life took an unexpected turn. Her desire to regain her lost bustline led Julie to give birth again, but this time to a business idea. Some of her friends had undergone plastic surgery to boost their bust, but Julie was concerned about the health risks and pain of silicone implants. But, it was silicone implants that gave her an idea. She reasoned if silicone inside a woman's breast plumped up her bustline, why couldn't a pad of silicone worn outside the body achieve the same result?

Determined to make the product for women, Julie borrowed $100,000 and set up shop in her garage, seeking technical advice from a friend, on how to design the product. The result was tear-resistant polyurethane pads that contain medical-grade silicone gel, which 'jiggle' like natural breasts and can be tucked inside any underwire bra or swimsuit. They called the product, Curves.

Launched in 1994, the timing was perfect. Controversy over the dangers of silicone implants was making headline news and many women were looking for a natural alternative to plastic surgery. Airing the product on TV and through mail order, within two years, gross sales topped $12million. Julie no longer works from her garage, instead she runs her company BodyLines from an office where her two children often visit her.

Her clients include top actresses and costume designers. 'Baywatch' costume designer Karen Braverman, says with Curves, you don't have to be voluptuous, you can just look that way.
Julie has some advice to give other budding entrepreneurs:

1. Have some knowledge of the product you're selling.
2. Don't rely on the opinions of friends and family, especially if they're not familiar with your product.
3. Research the market, talk to experts and put together a team of people who have the expertise you need.
4. Be prepared to work hard.
5. Julie donates a portion of each Curves sale to breast cancer.

She expects sales of $20million for her third year in business, from her uplifting idea.

A £2,500 Loan to Stock Market Value of £88million!
Name: Dylan Wilk.
Nationality: British.
Age: 20 yrs when started his business.
'Foolish' Idea: Selling computer games by mail-order.
Start-up Capital: A £2,500 loan from the Prince's Trust.

How Idea was Launched: For the first year, Dylan ran his Leeds-based mail-order company, Gameplay, on his own from home. He purchased games at competitive prices. Once he'd worked out the costs, he advertised the games, buying them in as people ordered them.

Sales: Entirely through mail order from advertising. Gameplay, now has a huge warehouse for its stock.

Earnings: The firm was floated on the stock market at the initial value of £88 million in August 1999. Dylan personally made £4 million from the deal.

No bank would lend money to Dylan Wilk, although they agreed his business plan was good. Instead, they advised him to return in 10 years time, because at 20 yrs, they said he was too young. So, Dylan applied to the Prince's Trust and they gave him a loan of £2,500.

Working from home, which was a flat, he telephoned all the major suppliers of computer games and shouted at them until they agreed to supply his business, Gameplay, at competitive prices. His flat was soon piled high with boxes of computer games, they were even stacked up in the bathroom. After about 7 months his mother started helping out. He continued working from home for the first year, advertising the games then buying them in as people placed orders.

Business was booming when Dylan suffered a major setback. A powerful business man started a business calling it Gameplay Ltd and issued a high court writ to stop Dylan trading. Dylan had a couple of months of hell, but he won the court case, because he'd been trading under that name for a year.

So, Dylan carried on expanding Gameplay for another 4 years, until August 1999, when the firm floated on the stock market for £88million, of which £4million went to Dylan, personally.

Selling Books Turnover More than £100million!

Name: Tim Waterstone.
Nationality: British.
Age: 52 yrs.
'Foolish' Idea: Selling books.
Start-up Capital: £6,000 of own money. Borrowed £75,000 under the Small Business Loan Guarantee Scheme and an extra £20,000 to top up.
How Idea was Launched: The start-up capital funded his first Waterstone's bookshop.
Sales: There are over 90 shops in Britain plus expanding chain in America.
Earnings: Turnover is more than £100million.

Tim Waterstone was chairman of W.H. Smiths American Company, until he was fired, because the company had lost a lot of money. So, Tim opened up the first of the Waterstone's bookshop chain.

He came from a typical lower middle-class family with absolutely no money, and had six children at the time of the sacking. Tim took all the money he had, which was £6,000, and put it into the business. Borrowed funds of £95,000 added to his own money, funded the first shop.

Tim has his own top ten tips to make a million:
1. You must learn to totally understand the finances and the way your business is run. Never let an accountant run your business. A business will crash if you are taken by surprise with a cash shortage, so always be obsessed with cashflow.
2. Spend your whole time looking forward. Always ask, how much cash are you going to need next year?
3. Keep the business simple. Make lines of communication short and concentrate on simple straightforward issues.
4. Always run a business you truly understand. Do what you are good at.

5. Motivate people instead of bossing them into action. Give people a happy atmosphere to work in.
6. Treat everyone you meet well - your staff, shareholders, customers, suppliers.
7. Don't try to get your own way all the time. Be prepared to concede smaller issues to win the war. Winning the war, is having the most successful, happy company possible.
8. Always be positive and dynamic, planning for an even greater and better future. Be bold.
9. Listen to other people's opinions, but at the end of the day, be clear what you're doing, and have the guts to follow your own intuition and make your own decisions.
10. Make sure your staff understand the rules and goals - then allow them to exercise responsibility and to have fun at doing things for themselves.

Following these rules, Tim Waterstone has built up the Waterstone's bookshop chain and exceeded well over £100million turnover.

Kid-friendly Frozen Food Bakes up a Fortune!

Name: Fran Lent.
Nationality: American.
Age: 42yrs.
'Foolish' Idea: Prepackaged meals which are healthy and to entice children to eat them, fun shaped and named. Start-up Capital: $130,000 life savings.
How Idea was Launched: Fran started her own frozen food company, Fran's Healthy Helpings, in 1997. She placed her products in about 300 independent stores.
Sales: Now, supermarket chains, such as Safeway and Albertson's sell the healthy TV dinners.
Earnings: Within 2 years, $3million-a-year, expecting revenues of $40million within the next 5 years.

Fran Lent's children, Bradley and Hannah, are her best critics. Fran, who used to work as a marketer for Del Monte Foods in San Francisco, didn't have time to prepare meals. However, her children wouldn't eat many of the prepackaged meals she dished up. And as a caring mother, she was unhappy about offering them meals loaded with sodium and fat.

So, using the family's $130,000 life savings, Fran began dreaming up her own prepackaged meals. She surrounded herself with other mums to create fun foods for kids. They made sure no artificial additives or preservatives were used, and baked ingredients instead of frying them. They gave all the foods kid-friendly names cutting and shaping the food for fun. Packs of Lucky Ducky Chicken are baked nuggets shaped like ducks, while Wacky Whale Pizzas are whale-shaped pies, containing low-fat cheese.

In 1997 Fran launched her company, Fran's healthy Helpings, placing the products in around 300 independent stores. Then supermarket chains started selling them. Fran's Healthy Helpings frozen food company, make healthy TV dinners that parents are happy to dish up and kids enjoy eating. Fran tests her products on her own kids, and other kids too. Cooking up fun meals, has created $3million-a-year with expected revenues of $40million within five years.

Off-beat Fashion Empire turns Rags to Riches!

Names: Angela McLean and Traci Egan.
Nationalities: Both American.
Ages: Angela, 33yrs. Traci not known.
'Foolish' Idea: Seeing discarded clothes as an untapped, off-beat fashion empire.
Start-up Capital: Approx $2,000
How Idea was Launched: The friends purchased designer outfits and haute couture fashions at yard and garage sales. They opened

their first store in a strip mall, with the attention-grabbing, 'Psycho Sisters Consignment Shops'. This store was followed by others.
Sales: Fashionable 'vintage' garments start at $1.99 and go up to $19.99. The stores sell to general public and also attract celebrities.
Earnings: Personal annual incomes are well over $100,000.

Angela McLean was astonished to discover designer outfits and haute couture fashions, being sold for next to nothing at yard and garage sales. It gave her an idea. She formed a partnership with her old college pal, Traci Egan, to open a boutique featuring stylish second-hand clothes. They hadn't decided on a name for their boutique when late one night on a trip to Atlanta they drove through a terrific storm.

Angela commented to Traci, that they must be crazy. Traci agreed and said they were, psycho. They thought it would be a great name and settled on, Psycho Sisters Consignment Shops. They went on a massive buying spree, spending hundreds of hard-earned dollars and ended up with twenty bulging boxes of second-hand clothes.

Angela, who has a degree in advertising, was working as a waitress at the time. She had her first credit card with a limit of one thousand five hundred dollars, which she used for advertising. They opened their first store in a strip mall, because the prices were low.

Today, each of the Psycho Sisters shops sell fashionable vintage garments from $1.99 to $19.99. Each shop is uniquely decorated with giant bumble bees hanging from the ceiling rubbing shoulders with fluffy feather boas. The walls boast Mardi Gras masks. The bold décor is all part of their careful marketing strategy which has paid off dividends.

All the garments they've hand-picked from yard and garage sales, are carefully laundered and repaired, ensuring they are all in top condition. The girls have plans to start their own affordable fashion label. Meanwhile, their shops are attracting celebrities, and Angela and Traci are enjoying annual incomes of well over $100,000's - all from selling discarded clothes.

Nail Polish Blossoms into a $10million Make-up Company!

Name: Dineh Mohajer.
Nationality: American.
Age: 24 years.
'Foolish' Idea: Funky coloured nail polish.
Start-up Capital: Cost of a few bottles of nail varnish.
How idea was Launched: Started company, Hard Candy. Took 4 new nail varnish colours, as samples to store, Fred Segal in LA. Sold instantly and store ordered 200 more bottles.
Sales: They also supplied smaller boutiques in LA. By the beginning of 1996, Hard Candy nail polish was going into all the big stores like Harrods, Havey Nichols and Saks. Sales are also by mail order.
Earnings: Company is worth over $10million.
Spin-offs: Developed new products for the Hard Candy range, eyeshadow sets and pencils.

Dineh Mohajer always mixed up her own nail polish to match the colour of her outfit. Her sister remarked on the many compliments people paid Dineh, many also asking where they could purchase nail polish in the colours she wore.

Dineh was set on becoming a doctor, but was so burnt out with studying she quit. Then her sister suggested she sell nail polish. Dineh teamed up with her boyfriend, Ben, and they started mixing colours. First was baby blue, made by mixing up dark blue with white varnish. Dineh took four samples - baby blue, sunshine yellow, lime green and lavender - to the department store, Fred Segal, in LA.

These four bottles of varnish sat on the counter, unpriced. A young girl spotted them and was so enthusiastic, the store buyer said they were $18 each. When the girl's mother bought all four bottles for her daugher, the buyer ordered 200 bottles - to be delivered tomorrow. It took four days to make the 200 bottles, in the kitchen, shaking and shaking the varnish until they'd blended and created their new colours. As fast as they delivered, the store re-ordered.

Using bottles bought from a beauty supplier, they made their packaging special, by decorating the tops of the bottles with cute rings from inside kids' goodie bags. They bought the entire stock and then had to start importing the rings from Taiwan.

Soon celebrities began wearing the nail varnish. This attracted the attention of the magazines, and Vogue, Elle and MTV picked up on it in the summer of 1995. By 1996, they were supplying Hard Candy nail polish to the big stores, Harvey Nichols, Harrods and Saks.

Next Hard Candy launched more products, eyepencils, mascara and eyeshadow sets with names like Rockstar and Techno. Dineh Mohajer has turned her passion for unusual coloured nail varnish into a company worth over $10million.

Part Two
30 Great Businesses For You To Think About!

How to Buy a Business For Less Than £1,000

As a short cut to making money, buying a business is often a quicker and more profitable alternative to setting one up.

Purchasing someone else's business need be no more expensive than starting up your own. In fact, in some situations it can even be cheaper, with the added advantage that you will be earning income from the business from the day you start.

How can it be cheaper? Obviously it will cost you money to buy the business in the first place, but because you are trading from day one, you can avoid most of the costs involved in business set up and can pay off your initial outlay much sooner.

Most people think that buying a business is extremely expensive. This is not necessarily the case: there are situations where an existing business can be bought for less than £1,000. If you've got more cash to invest that's a bonus - but you can manage on £1,000 if you look hard enough and are prepared to wait.

Nobody is saying that you are going to buy a lucrative, thriving business for a ridiculously low sum. But buying a business from the 'bargain basement' where few major players are found, you can buy a business at low cost, and possibly at much less than it is actually worth. Here's how to find and purchase a bargain business.

What Type of Business Can You Buy?

On such a tight budget, choice will be limited. Businesses 'going for a song' tend to be small one-man firms often operated at home.

They tend to be services that carry little or no stock, which further depresses the price. They are sometimes shops on lease, where very little of the lease is left, or perhaps in a poor position. Often they are businesses which have been rendered obsolete by modern technology in some way.

Unfortunately you aren't going to get 'state of the art' for £1,000, but this doesn't actually matter. The business can still be extremely good value, and even if you only operate it for a year or two it may still bring you a good return for the money invested.

Typical examples of 'ultra cheap' businesses are:
* window cleaning rounds;
* small, often run down, shops;
* mobile shops and catering trailers;
* delivery rounds (e.g. milk, vegetables);
* market stalls;
* kiosks;
* craft businesses;
* taxis (occasionally in less busy areas);
* home based services, like carpet cleaning, security window engraving.

Of course, not all of these are available for a few pounds, and not all are run down or very basic, although these do exist. Don't just confine yourself to these suggestions as there are other types available.

Where to Find Cheap Businesses

Cheap businesses are not plentiful so you need to know where to look. Firstly, try Business Transfer Agents. These are like estate agents, except they buy and sell businesses. You will find these in your local Yellow Pages. Most have particulars of businesses and maybe even a regular listing or newspaper they can send you. Ask to be put on their mailing list and specify you are interested only in low cost businesses.

The next good source of cheap businesses is your local press. Most newspapers have a 'businesses for sale and wanted' section. Here cheap businesses are advertised directly by their owners (i.e. not through agents). Often only a box number is given and you need to write for further details. It costs very little to do this, but give an absolute minimum away about yourself when you write. You want the seller to want to sell to you, and not find yourself in a seller's market.

The weekly national newspaper Daltons Weekly also contains hundreds of businesses for sale. As with transfer agents these are predominantly more expensive businesses, but there are some bargains available. Look carefully in the classified advertisement sections.

Finally, there is nothing to stop you placing a 'business wanted' advertisement in your local press, Daltons Weekly or even the Exchange & Mart magazine. State that you will consider purchasing any up and running business for less than £1,000 (or whatever you have).

It is quite reasonable to approach the owner of any small business (for sale or not) and offer to buy. All businesses are for sale - it depends on the price and the current mental state/situation of the owner. This might meet with an indignant response, but it costs nothing to try, and there are a surprising number of small home businesses all over the country whose owners wouldn't normally think of selling such a cheap business, but might be tempted by your offer of up to £1,000. In fact, you could well offer less and find someone who urgently needs to sell!

Basic Checks

When a suitable bargain business comes up, ask for written particulars, then go to see the business, or see the owner if there are no premises involved. Before you go, make up a list of questions you want to ask to build up an accurate picture of what you are being offered. For example:
* what does the business do?
* how long has it been running?
* what are the minimum and the average weekly takings?
* why are they selling?
* where is stock obtained from?
* what is the gross profit margin?

Don't consider buying any businesses that aren't up and running. For example, a kit of tools needed to run a certain service - but which the owner has never actually advertised or run - is not a going concern.

Surf the Net for Profit
20 Ways to Make Money from the Internet

Have you discovered the Internet yet and the millions of business opportunities it offers? Don't worry, you don't need to be a computer boffin to get involved. In fact, you don't even have to have a computer and modem to profit from the Net!

There are many simple sales opportunities, for example, servicing Internet companies. If you do have the basic equipment there are plenty of ways to profit from people all over the world, whether they are on line or not. And if you know the Web coding language HTML (which can be learned from the many books that are available on the subject) the world of opportunity opens out even more.

Above all, there's no need to be scared of the Internet. Most of the opportunities here require only a basic grounding in the workings of the World Wide Web and e-mail. Here are our top 20 ways for you to surf the Net for profit!

1. Finding Internet Customers

The number of people using the Internet continues to grow, as they begin to realise the full benefits it brings. Internet Service Providers (ISPs) are competing desperately to sign up customers, which has resulted in a need for middle men to sign up non-Net surfers on behalf of the company, and/or attract customers away from their current service provider. You'll either receive a payment per person you sign up, or will get a percentage of their subscription for as long as they use the service. Finding new customers is not difficult. Word of mouth will generate a certain amount of custom, so inform friends and work colleagues; explain what they'll gain from going on line, plus the benefits of your particular service provider. Business customers will be more lucrative. Target firms likely to benefit from the Internet, attracting them via direct mail shots, leaflet drops, newspaper ads and articles.

2. Renting out Web Space

Clients will pay to have a site on the World Wide Web, earning money for the large Internet service providers who rent out nearly all Web space. For smaller operators there is a market for buying Web space and 'subletting' it at a profit. For example, you could buy Web space for £x per megabyte and rent it out to a company at double the price. First find a reliable provider of Web space. (Note: some services offer a certain amount of free Web space for your own personal use, which you may lose by renting it on.) Next you need to promote your business to potential customers. You can set up a Web site to do this, highlighting the benefits of your service (quality of service, speed of access, reliability or price, for example) and giving testimonials from satisfied customers. Also, target non-Web using companies by direct mail and other means, explaining the benefits of being on line.

3. On line Classifieds

The World Wide Web is essentially one great big virtual advertising hoarding, but it's costly to purchase space, and many firms and individuals either don't want or can't afford a Web site. However, they may wish to pay to put a small classified ad on the Net. Setting up a Web site featuring lots of small classified ads is a lucrative opportunity. You can charge a certain rate per word, for a standard run of a week or a fortnight. All you then have to do is update the site when necessary. As well as basic classifieds you can charge extra for boxed ads, links to customers' own Web sites and so on. It's a good idea to charge reduced rates initially in order to get your first few customers. To advertise the site, leave messages in the classified ads news groups.

4. Internet Job Centre
For someone desperately looking for a job, it would be an excellent idea to advertise their skills and experience on the World Wide Web. It would probably reach for more firms and cost far less than mailing out CVs direct. However, Web browsing firms looking for prospective employees would need to know where to look. This is where you come in, with an Internet job centre. Get people to send in their CVs and charge them for posting up a few brief details regarding their experience, qualifications and the work they are looking for. Interested companies could then contact you, with you charging a fee for sending out each person's full CV. Try to group people so that companies can find what they are looking for quickly. You can also offer a service to companies trying to fill a post, matching up people with their particular job requirements. This would be useful for firms without the time or equipment for Net surfing. You need to make your site well known to companies. As well as advertising your presence via the Internet, contact the personnel departments of large companies and use mail shots to attract non-Net users.

5. Monitoring Web Sites
Businesses are always keen to find out what their competitors are doing on line. You can charge clients for keeping an eye on certain

Web sites - the information featured, number of 'hits' (people visiting the site), and changes made - and presenting it as a report which shows how the company could update their own site to make it better than their competitors. You can charge upwards of £20 per hour for this service, plus telephone expenses, but you need to keep your customer informed of what you've been up to. Use targeted e-mail, letters, ads in the various Internet magazines, plus your own Web site, to attract custom.

6. Web Page Design and Copywriting

When companies go on line it helps that their site is attractively designed and well laid out. A site that's interesting to look at and not too complicated, with plenty to offer the reader, will keep people coming back for more, so many companies will require the services of a Web page designer in order to maximise their Web potential. As well as artistic talent you'll need to be familiar with HTML, the coding language used by the Web, but there are lots of books on the subject available. Approach design companies, who may be looking for people with Web designing experience. Another good marketing method is to contact companies already on the Net and (tactfully) offer to redesign their pages.

7. Copywriting

To really make a Web page or an e-mail sales letter sell, it needs to be snappily and persuasively written. For this reason, there are excellent opportunities for copywriters. Web site copy needs to be short, sharp, keeping the reader's attention, gradually attracting them through the pages of the site and prodding them towards purchasing that particular product or service. This is not quite as straightforward as copywriting a standard mailshot or sales letter, but several helpful books are available. You can charge by the hour, by the project or by the page.

8. Public Relations

Organisations use public relations for a variety of reasons - boosting their company profile, beating off competition and increasing prestige, as well as selling products - and maintaining a strong Internet presence can be an important part of this. There is money to be made in Internet based PR, handling the on line PR requirements for a variety of businesses. You need to build up a list of contacts and publications, their editors and journalists, and their e-mail addresses. Directories with the contact numbers of UK based publications are available, some in computer disk format. You can then issue press releases by e-mail as well as utilising Web sites, charging either by the release or on a retainer basis.

9. Publishing

Whether you require a little light hearted reading or some serious information, you might be able to get it in the form of an on line publication. This is another lucrative area of the Internet you can get involved in. The simplest form of publishing is to issue small newsletters by e-mail. Alternatively, you could set up an in depth Web based publication, which will involve more work, but you can charge more for it. You don't necessarily have to charge - by carrying advertising a free publication should make a profit. The content is up to you, although business, financial and sex related magazines are popular. Include things like up to the minute news, competitions, interviews, features and reviews of other relevant Internet sites. Charges will depend how long the publication is and how specialised the information is, but you can make customers pay by using a password system, or by taking credit/debit card details. Don't forget to advertise your publication extensively on the Net, and use mailing lists to mailshot potential readers and contributors.

10. Lonely Hearts and Personal Sites

The Internet is a great way for unattached people to communicate, perhaps aided by the anonymity it offers. However, it's not the sort of place that encourages people getting together, so there's a great demand for lonely hearts and personal services that operate via the Web or e-mail. Feature short descriptions of each person, along with what they are looking for, and encourage people to contact you, paying a small fee to see someone's details and picture. Don't give out contact details though - if the other person is interested they can pass on a message to confirm a 'date'. If you wish you can charge people a membership fee to join your service. Vetting your clients will help improve their chances of finding a suitable partner, boosting your success rates and attracting more customers. Advertise your site in newspapers, magazines and through specialised mailing lists, as well as on the Net itself.

11. Games and Competitions

People love games and competitions, which is why they are so profitable. The simplest form of Net competition is a quiz - music, general knowledge and films are popular - where people can obtain the questions by e-mail. It is possible to set up virtually any kind of competition if you use your imagination. Prizes can be obtained by asking companies (not only those on the Net) to donate a prize in return for advertising space, with profits being earned by selling additional ad space, plus mailing lists of customers and advertisers. Dedicated games services are also popular. Software companies now have facilities to play their games over the Net, but can be slow. Far better to set up a dedicated game server (with hard/software that allows people to play against one another, such at BT's WirePlay), charging by the hour. Rent space from your local Net service provider, offering a dedicated game service with favourites like Doom or Quake. Your charges will therefore be added to customers' monthly on line bills from their providers. If you don't have the necessary technical expertise to set up a game or competition site contact your service provider - they may help you in return for a percentage of your charges.

12. Information Sites

Do you have a special interest or area of expertise? If so, you could set up an information site on the Net. More and more people are making significant cash doing this. It should carry exciting and enjoyable features to draw in your captive audience, who can then be encouraged to register for your information areas. These are protected by a password which you only give out when your customer has completed the relevant forms. You could write the site yourself, or get writers to contribute articles. Remember you can make more cash by featuring adverts too. Publicise your site via other Web pages and links from those pages, and mailshot organisations who may be interested in your service.

13. Teaching

Anyone with a good grounding in computing and the Internet will be able to earn a healthy income passing on their knowledge to others. Businesses will want to know to set up on the Internet, how to develop a Web site and how best to make money. Home users will want to benefit from all the different areas of the Net - particularly leisure and fun pages - as well as discovering how to go on line. You could start off teaching at home, or in companies' own offices. For a particularly up market business related course, where you include lunch and an expert and/or guest speaker, you can charge well upwards of £100 per day. If you have little computing knowledge but are good at organising, you could hire teachers and just handle the school's marketing, booking and admin. You'll still pocket the profits!

14. 'How To .....' Newsletters and Disks

A helpful service for organisations looking to either set up or improve a Web site is to provide an information service or newsletter analysing what the most successful sites are, how many people access them, and what actually makes them successful. You can charge around £100 per year for a basic five page monthly newsletter, although it depends how specialised your information is. You could also produce CDs and disks featuring examples of Web sites, along with links, plus Internet software and more. Don't forget to ask permission before using anyone's Web site as an example, although you can charge for the privilege, since the organisation might view it as a good source of advertising. Putting ads in magazines and setting up your own Web site will be the most effective way of marketing this service.

15. Bartering on the Net
Bartering is a great way of saving money, and is enjoying a huge growth in popularity thanks to the advantages offered by the Internet. Contact your local service provider and set up a newsgroup where people can advertise goods wanted and offered. You act as the middle man, putting together buyer and seller and taking a commission on each transaction. The club can be promoted via press releases to Internet-related magazines and on the Net itself.

16. On-line Auctions
It's possible to set up instant on-line auctions via the Internet or your local bulletin board. You can sell anything you like, although the best items are computer and electrical equipment. Contact local shops to obtain stock. Stress that not only will they sell their goods quickly, they'll get free advertising too. Using a Web site you can display details of goods, along with a picture, the last bid received, the amount the bid can be increased by (£5 is a good amount), plus the cost of sending the goods to the winning bidder. Accept new bids by e-mail and update your site accordingly. Set a two-week limit per auction, so that the highest bid at the end of the fortnight gets the goods. You can then pass on the details of the winner to the shop, who will send the items out and pay you your commission (at least 10 percent of the sale).

17. Installing Internet Software
Anyone who is up to speed with Internet technology can make a good living installing software. Although the basics are fairly simple, getting the right configurations and settings can be time consuming, so you'll help organisations save time and money by providing this service. You'll need to know how to set up the most popular software - Web browsers and Internet-related software - and help with any problems they encounter afterwards. Advertise your service to local businesses via direct mail and leaflet drops. Also you

could approach computer stores to pass on your leaflet, or perhaps hire you to install their products.

18. Internet Consultancy

If a company wanted to know how to set up on the Internet, how to market itself via the Net, or how to get the most out of it, they'd probably turn to an Internet consultancy. Depending on the service provided they might have to pay between £25 and £100 per hour for the information - precisely why consultancy is such a good earner. You can either offer a general service or specialise in areas such as the Web, advertising, marketing or public relations.

19. X-rated Sites

There's no doubt about it: sex sells. You've probably heard horror stories about computer porn, but as long as you steer clear of anything illegal you can make a lot of money from 'sex sites'. Lingerie, books magazines and toys sell very well, as buyers and sellers benefit from the cloak of anonymity the Net provides. These goods are easy to sell - put a catalogue on the Web and open a 'cardholder not present' account with Access and Visa to accept credit card details.

20. Net Security

The nightmare of hackers gaining access to sensitive files, changing codes and spreading computer viruses is one shared by many organisations that use the Internet. Net security, although complex, offers substantial rewards to those able to install security-protecting software and/or assess companies' computer systems and recommend ways of preventing unauthorised access. A good way of generating clients is to collect stories of security break-ins and mailshot companies offering your services. Do security reviews for local firms to generate testimonials, as these will be a brilliant advertisement. This is one of the most lucrative Net-related opportunities: you can charge upward of £300 a day for this work.

Video Wills
The Camcorder Based Business With HUGE Potential!

If you own a camcorder you have any number of money making opportunities at your disposal. Here is one opportunity that is fun and extremely lucrative: making video wills.

What are video wills?
They are an ideal addition to the standard 'Last Will and Testament'. A fantastic opportunity for someone to make a personal statement to their families and loved ones, communicating feelings that written wills do not express.

What do video wills consist of?
Making video wills requires a talent for filming and editing, but it is enjoyable work and fairly straightforward. You will need to travel to various locations to film, such as the client's home, the place they were married in, or any other location with personal relevance and happy memories. A soundtrack could be included, perhaps featuring the client's favourite songs, and the video could even be supplemented with treasured photographs. (Note: you won't have to pay to use music over 100 years old on which copyright has expired. However, anything more recent you will need to obtain permission to use and will probably have to pay a fee for.)

Why do clients value video wills?
The videos are certainly an excellent means of recording a final statement, although by working with clients on a more long term basis you can produce a film that will have great sentimental value, encompassing all kinds of places, memories and people. They are of great posterity and historical value too, being ideal ways for descendants and friends to remember someone. Those who live far away - who perhaps will be unable to visit the client before they die, or may have difficulty visiting the client's last resting place - will find comfort in a personal film which can be easily sent all over the world.

Will i require legal experience?

You won't require any in-depth legal knowledge, as video wills do not actually compete with written wills in legal terms. Written wills remain the most important factor in litigation. The videos simply act as an accompaniment, communicating personal feelings rather than legal statements.

How do i film each video?

It is vital to put new clients at ease. Encourage them to think about what they want to say beforehand, along with the locations, family memorabilia and music they want to include. If necessary, give hints about what to say and where to film. When you do the filming, ensure that the client's family will be out for the day. To enable your client to get used to the camera let them have a couple of dummy runs before filming. Then, when complete, go through the tape to ensure your client is satisfied. Look towards producing an hour long film, featuring the client reading his testimony at home or in familiar surrounds, intercut with other speech, locations and so on. Add titles where necessary, not forgetting to include the name of your video company.

How do i market this service?

It is a good idea to advertise this service in local or national newspapers. Get some leaflets printed too - put them in shop windows and circulate them to social clubs and solicitors. You may be able to get trade directly from life assurance companies and solicitors, negotiating a commission on each video sold. How much you charge your client will depend on your filming time and expenses, but you can set a basic rate of £250 for producing a one hour video. If you provide a quality product with great sentimental value you will undoubtedly earn far more as your reputation spreads.

Child Identification Services

The summer's biggest news item was the incredibly hot weather, but sadly it was also a season that brought a series of assaults on young children. This has led to a heightened awareness of children's vulnerability, and has highlighted the need for a child identification service.

Ensuring Peace of Mind

The child identification service could bring peace of mind to millions of worried parents wishing to ensure their own child's safety, and alleviate the horror and panic experienced when youngsters go missing. It offers immediate information on personal details - particularly an up to date photograph - which is of vital importance to police, security staff, the media and other search agencies, and this forms the basis of the service you can offer.

A Simple Service, With Massive Potential

The advantage of the business is that it is simple, logical and profitable with low start up costs, requires no previous experience to run, and has already proved to be a massive success in the US.

The core of the service is that provision of a credit card sized, hard plastic identity card, which is heat sealed and contains the child's name, colour photograph, physical details and address. Actually manufacturing the cards is very easy, the equipment is very transportable and the process very quick, so you will be able to travel around and issue cards on the spot.

On the reverse of the card, there is room to provide a check list of immediate action in an emergency. This kind of information can be invaluable in helping distraught parents or guardians to focus clearly in a crisis.

The list will include instructions to:

* * Call the police or appropriate security staff immediately and show them the identity card (if necessary the card can be instantly photocopied to supply any number of searchers)
* * Alert friends and neighbours
* * Organise an immediate search
* * Check the child's favourite play areas or their friend's homes. Also included will be relevant agency telephone numbers.

A Community Friendly Service

Obviously the service should be marketed to parents, but since it is likely that their children will also be cared for by other adults, the scheme offers multi sale potential. The low cost community friendly aspect of the scheme should be stressed, providing a proactive and pre-emptive rather than reactive service, whose end product will hopefully never be used.

The Customer Base

The customer base is enormous and initial contact could be made by mail shots to key people in schools, playgroups and day care centres. You could also contact police stations and fire departments, local government agencies responsible for child welfare, or even get sponsorship from local businesses.

Other young people's organisations such as Brownies and Guides, Cubs and Scouts, churches and sports teams would also be interested. The natural sense of responsibility and concern for young people by leaders of these organisations will encourage take up of the service.

A Highly Transportable Service

Because the manufacturing cost of the identity cards is relatively low, they can be sold at a very attractive price, so you could offer the group a commission and still make a healthy profit.

It is likely that in any one group there may be over 20 potential customers, with a good chance many of them would require more than one card, but because the card making equipment is very easy to transport, they can be accommodated very quickly.

There are a wide range of sales opportunities in locations where families are to be found, with shopping centres, cinemas and leisure centres offering fertile bases for the identification service. Other favourable venues are school fetes, market areas, theme parks, seaside resorts or anywhere visited by responsible and aware adults.

Ongoing Profit Potential

A further increase in profit can be generated by regularly updating a child's card - just think how much youngsters' features change as they develop. It is also useful to remember also that many areas of the country are heavily populated by people of an ethnic origin and that cards produced in an appropriate language would also benefit sales, backed up by complementary promotional literature.

Areas of Concern

A possible area of concern is the potential for misuse of the personal data supplied for the card. It should be made clear in any promotional material or personal presentation that the information supplied is strictly confidential and will not be used in any way to form a database. However, if you promote the service correctly the overriding concern for the safety of children should ensure the success of the scheme.

How To Give Your Product Away And Still Make A Fortune

What is the secret of business success? You may think it is to sell your product at the highest price to the most people. Think again - you can actually make more money by giving your product away!

The Secret of Successful Business

This is a technique which reveals the secret of practically every successful business. It relies on repeat sales, built up from the initial purchase of the product. The problem of generating the initial purchase is overcome if the product is free, so eventually you should be left with legions of loyal customers and you can hardly fail to make a fortune.

The Benefits of Repeat Sales
Before we explain this in more detail, take the example of Coca Cola - a company whose business has been based on the success of basically one drink. How far would the company have grown if they had sold a can to everyone in the world, but nobody bought another one?

The success of the company is, of course, built on repeat sales. Coca Cola drinkers don't just buy one can, they buy lots of them, over years and years. The success of the business depends on gaining a customer, providing them with a product they are satisfied with, and then reaping the benefits of repeat sales.

Brand and Company Loyalty
This doesn't just apply to consumable, low cost items. A motorcar is a very expensive purchase, and an infrequent one. Yet the fortunes of motor manufacturers are dependent on selling not just one car to a customer, but several over their lifetime.

Why does the Ford company continue to prosper, and why is the Ford Escort still a number one seller? Those with rose tinted spectacles would like to think it is because Ford produce the best, most reliable car with the greatest range of features and benefits, at the best price. Most independent observers would differ from this view, pointing to the cars coming from Japan and Europe.

At one time, however, Ford did produce this type of car, and this is the point. Once customers start to buy from a supplier they are notoriously hard to move. Put simply, if they bought Ford last time they are likely to buy it again, irrespective of any arguments to the contrary.

The Initial Sale

The phenomenon of brand and company loyalty is very important and explains why companies spend such huge sums of money in order to persuade someone to try out their product. The initial sale forms only part of the benefit of advertising, and is often little more than incidental. If MacDonalds only encouraged people to enter their restaurants once, never to return, their advertising expenditure would be wasted and they would quickly go out of business.

Gaining Customers

So what does this mean to you? Whatever business you are in, it is likely that it actually costs you money to gain a customer. There may well be no profit in the initial sale, which will be swallowed up in marketing costs, whether advertising, direct mail, telesales, personal representation, or whatever.

The fact is that this initial sale is crucial, in order to make subsequent sales which make a profit. Or is it?

Giving your product away, in the context of the above, seems to make sense.

Here is an example. Assume that you produce and market a food supplement which sells by mail for £5. Your product cost is 75 pence, and postage and packing another 50p. The gross profit margin is quite high, although this will be eroded by advertising costs when trying to attract new customers. It could cost between £5 and £10 to attract the new customer, which you would hope to make back when people re-order the product.

Here's an alternative - offer the product free of charge. The cost to you including postage and packing is £1.25........ much less than it would cost to make a 'sale'. Also, the take up rate will be far higher. You will have a massive database of people who have now sampled your product, and hopefully benefited from it.

Advertise For Free
You may have spotted a flaw in this argument. What about advertising costs? You still have to inform potential customers that they can have a sample for free. Well, yes you do, but you don't necessarily have to pay for it. Get others to do it for free.

Here is just one way of doing it. A recent copy of The Mail on Sunday carried an article about a young man who had built his video tape business to a turnover in excess of £2 million using this method. One of the main methods he had used to achieve this was giving away his product free.

For example, a series of his products was aimed at anglers. He contacted one of the major angling magazines and told them that he had several thousand videos to give away to its readers. They were naturally delighted, because being able to make such an offer helps to sell magazines. The magazine featured the offer heavily and it was a tremendous success.

Although the initial result was a cost incurred, the entrepreneur was able to enclose literature promoting associated videos with the free one. This resulted in many thousands of pounds worth of sales.

Potential Uses and Spin-offs
You will probably be able to think of many potential uses and spin-offs from this technique. It can be adapted to many different products and markets. Perhaps you have something to sell which could benefit from this approach.

Don't forget the next time you are pondering over how to sell more of your product, consider giving it away instead. It's a lot easier and it could definitely be more profitable in the long run.

Two Profitable Hobbies
Enjoy Your Hobby and Make Money From it Too!

If you're looking for a part time extra money making project, why not join those lucky people who earn pounds from pursuing their hobby? Or to put it another way, if you're looking for a new hobby, then why not go for one that will actually make you money, rather than become a drain on your resources? Here are our suggestions for two profitable hobby projects that you can enjoy as you earn.

1. Antiques and Collectibles
If you like discovering old treasures this is one area you'll find both fascinating and massively profitable. It's hard to decide whether it's too interesting to be a business or too profitable to be a hobby! Even better, you don't need to be a big antiques buff to get started in a small way.

The secret of success with antiques and collectibles is to buy cheap and sell at a mark up. So, for example, you could buy your stock from cheap locations such as junk shops and car boot sales and sell it at the smartest, most expensive antiques and collectors fairs you can find!

You're bound to make money, if only because sellers at car boot sales seriously undervalue their treasures while people are prepared, indeed expect, to pay much more in the plush surroundings of an antiques fair.

You can't expect to become an antiques expert in every subject overnight, so it's best to choose an area to specialise in. Most dealers do this - by having a thorough knowledge of one area they are able to spot little known treasures which they can buy for a few pounds and maybe sell for hundreds.

Easy areas to start in are pottery, glassware, jewellery and ephemera (printed collectibles). If you're working on a limited budget then don't be limited to the 'over 100 years old' rule which applies to most antiques. Collectibles, which are interesting items of any age, are just as profitable and there are loads of desirable collectible items from the 1950s and 60s!

Whatever area you decide to deal in, it pays to buy authoritative books and guides so you'll know what to look for. The monthly 'Antique Dealers and Collectors Guide' will give you a good background to most subjects. To subscribe call 01442 876661. For details of fairs you could attend, try 'British Antiques Fairs' (published annually).

2. Toy Making
There are few things more rewarding than making children's toys. If you like working with your hands you can turn this into a very nice little business, quite apart from the enjoyment of making unique handmade toys for your children or grandchildren and their friends.

First, decide exactly what you are going to make. Good choices are either soft toys (dolls and teddy bears are a favourite), or wooden toys. Toys made from carved, natural wood are very fashionable at the moment.

With toy making you'll find you don't have to start from scratch. There are several companies that sell plans, patterns, all the bits and pieces you'll need to make toys and even kits of parts too. Some of these are listed later.

Always obtain supplies that carry 'CE' European safety approval and use a fair degree of common sense as regards safety. Obviously, if the toy is for fairly young children, it shouldn't have any small parts, shouldn't contain anything sharp (use glue instead of nails and similar), and should only use non-toxic paints.

Once you have made a small stock of toys you can turn to selling. You should find plenty of demand from friends and relations, but you might want to go for something more organised - craft fairs, market stalls and Sunday markets are all possibilities. Also consider selling through toy shops and craft shops on a commission basis. If you like, you could even donate some of your profits to your favourite children's charity!

Sources of books, kits and parts for toy making: W Hobby Ltd, Knight's Hill Square, London SE27 OHH Tel: 020 8761 4244 Web: www.hobby.uk.com Fred Aldous Ltd, 37 Lever Street, Manchester M60 1UX Tel: 0161 236 2477 Web: www.fredaldous.co.uk

Bussing in the Business
Making Money from Second-hand Buses

When Cliff Richard and his gang went on their summer holidays in the 60s, little did they know they would spark off an excellent business opportunity decades later.

Today, buying up second-hand double decker buses represents a profitable sales opportunity and can even provide a new career.

A number of second-hand buses are now on the market for as little as £2,000. These can be refurbished and operated as travelling exhibition centres, showrooms or shops on behalf of certain clients.

Travelling the exhibition circuit can provide a lucrative source of income. For example, there are numerous computer fairs throughout the year, so if your client was a computer company, you would set up your bus and operate it as a mobile computer exhibition centre on behalf of your client. You may be able to set up an exclusive service on behalf of a single client, or work for different clients at different times of the year.

There are various aspects to the service you could provide. You could merely buy and sell second-hand buses to interested buyers, perhaps refurbishing them on their behalf. Or you could offer an owner/driver service, with you travelling with the bus at all times and providing care and maintenance. You may even be required to refurbish your bus to create extra berths to accommodate extra staff.

Since the exhibition circuit extends beyond the UK into Europe, by offering an owner/driver service you could end up with a real busman's holiday.

The first step is to get hold of a bus, so approach bus companies across the UK, and also keep an eye on the specialist trade magazines. Next, you will have to refurbish the bus, so do some research to find the best and cheapest source of refitters around.

Setting up the service is not prohibitively expensive. By looking for the best deal, it is possible to buy and sell a bus in suitable condition for £2,000.

There are also ways of avoiding the cost of refurbishment. When you have bought your bus and marketed your service to companies, it is likely you will have a few interested clients. By quoting a fee inclusive of refurbishment costs and organising the refurbishment yourself, you will have saved yourself the initial investment cost and also taken the organisational pressure off the company, making them more likely to purchase your service.

Another option is to approach your local TEC and Enterprise Agency. They may have sources of fitters and mechanics who will be able to supply you with free labour to work on the bus as part of their work experience.

It is useful, although not completely necessary, to have some knowledge of bus mechanics and maintenance. What is vital is that you keep the bus in tip top condition inside and out at all times.

There are many different kinds of companies you can approach, but try to concentrate on those which are more likely to be involved in trade fairs, such as companies selling expensive consumer goods, including computers. Try going along to a trade fair and approaching companies, or leave them your promotional literature and follow up later with a phone call.

The fees you charge should be based upon what you would require as your weekly salary, plus running costs, depreciation, and any refurbishment costs. This will probably be far in excess of £1,000 per week.

Since the cost to companies of buying in their own staff and paying a one off cost to set up their own exhibition stand is probably much higher, you should find that companies will be very interested in your service.

Carry On Camping
Setting Up Your Own Campsite

If you're after a rewarding rural lifestyle and a lucrative business at the same time, consider setting up your own campsite.

More and more families are choosing to start the summer holiday by throwing a tent, sleeping bags and camping stove into the car and heading off for a campsite. Camping and caravanning is a hugely popular pastime here in the UK, and many rural entrepreneurs are making a good living by catering for this growing market.

Opening your own campsite is a great way to grab a slice of the market for yourself. You get to enjoy the outdoor life in a scenic area, and rather than going out to find your customers, they come to you.

At its most basic, a campsite can be just a grassy field with a toilet and sink in the corner. Many farmers and country dwellers simply install lavatories and wash basins in an old shed and open up their land to campers. They spend half an hour every day collecting fees, leaving the rest of the day free for other activities. No expensive marketing is needed beyond a basic sign outside and a listing in the phone book and tourist information centre, and the only upkeep necessary is cleaning the toilets, emptying the rubbish and cutting the grass.

Camp Shops, Bars, Saunas and other facilities all help to boost revenue
While certainly a nice little earner, it's no fortune maker. By following the US blueprint you could turn the concept into a truly lucrative business. American campground owners have realised that while some campers don't mind roughing it in a field, others prefer the relative comfort of somewhere with hot showers, a swimming pool, a bar and a shop. By providing high quality amenities and impressing their own personalities onto their sites, owners have turned modest earners into extremely profitable franchises.

The key to US success has been to cater for a variety of travellers by offering a mix of tent sites, RV hookups and on site caravans and cabins. Their fairly high charges (around £8 - £18 per person/pitch per night; slightly more for a cabin) are justified by providing quality facilities, many of which provide additional sources of income. Large, clean bathhouses with plenty of clean toilets, basins and hot showers are essential. Camp shops, swimming pools, kitchens, launderettes, games rooms, telephone boxes and even saunas, bars and mini golf courses are frequently added, which all help to attract customers and generate a substantial boost in revenue.

If you're attracted by the rural life and dream of setting up a campsite, the first step is to find somewhere suitably large, flat and well drained, with space for a minimum of 20 pitches. The most profitable sites tend to be situated close to beauty spots and places of interest. If there are no toilets and washing facilities on site, you'll need to have them installed. Insurance cover is another expense.

Getting a loan to finance this type of business isn't always as easy as it should be. Some bank managers are unimpressed by campsites because of the relatively modest profits they make. However, the site will be covering most of your own living expenses (housing, utilities, etc.) so it is important to point this out. For your own benefit, don't forget the joys of living in beautiful countryside and earning a living in one of the most relaxed and rewarding ways possible.

Crime Scene Clean Up

It was while working as a crime reporter back in 1994 that Ray Barnes, of Fallston in Maryland, hit on a way to earn big money in his own business.

An elderly man had just killed himself with a shotgun, but no-one was in a rush to clean it up. Ray, who was armed with a strong constitution, stepped in. He got down on his hands and knees with a bucket and sponge and cleansed, disinfected and deodorised the area. He was paid handsomely, which set his mind thinking.

He knew, from his line of work, that one question relatives of the dead always asked was: who will clean up the remains? In partnership with his wife Louise, a cleaner, Ray developed a powerful stain cleaning solution and decided to go into business.

It took a few months to get hold of some full face respirators and disposable body suits, along with the licences to transport and dispose of biohazardous material. But once Ray put the word about with police departments that he was available, the phone did not stop ringing.

As the only people around offering such a service, Ray and his wife never turn jobs down. The business, Crime Scene Cleanup, has expanded to take on 23 part time employees in Atlanta, Philadelphia and Washington, with 13 fully kitted out trucks emblazoned with a fingerprint emblem. The rate of three murders an hour in the US is enough to keep them busy, and business is so good that the company's turnover is set to top $6 million this year.

While few people envy Ray in his work, most would not mind his earnings. His rates are $265 for the first hour (about £165) and $200 (£125) for each hour thereafter, paid for by either the police department or the relatives of the deceased. Since the work must be carried out to legal forensic guidelines, jobs take an average of four hours but can run into tens of thousands of dollars - enough for Ray to run a Rolls Royce and buy a multi million dollar home. Not for everyone, this, but it shows you that there are lots of ways to make money, once you start thinking.

Bargain Brief: Bicycles

What you need to know about bicycles!
Cycling is going through something of a boom time with plenty of demand for both new and used cycles. Bicycles, particularly mountain bikes, are highly profitable items, so this is an area of business that can be strongly recommended.

You may, on the other hand, just want to buy discount bikes for yourself and your family, in which case reading this section should prove useful.

Another advantage of selling bicycles is that as well as being profitable in their own right, customers are often also interested in buying other consumer goods, so if you offer several products then you will enjoy a high level of repeat and recommendation business can be enjoyed.

The main disadvantage to this trade is that cycles are very bulky to store and sell, so you will need plenty of space. Some basic mechanical knowledge would also be an advantage, for safety reasons.

Where to buy bikes
Trade warehouses offer cycles at a fraction of shop prices, especially if you can buy five or ten machines at once. Also, try auctions, classified ads, car boot and garage sales, and looking in magazines such as Dealer and Exchange and Mart. Be especially careful that you are not offered stolen stock.

What to buy
DO BUY:
* New cycles (especially surplus stock and catalogue returns)
* Used cycles if they are in tip top condition
* Well known brand names such as Raleigh, Townsend, British Eagle, Giant etc.
* Cycles in fashionable colours
* Mountain bikes and racing bikes.
* Children's cycles are always top sellers, especially in the pre-Christmas period (October - December).
DON'T BUY:
* Used bikes in shabby condition
* Unbranded or little known brands, especially cheap Chinese imports
* Ladies' bikes (the demand is quite limited)

How to check a bicycle

1. If the cycle is new, do not unpack or assemble it. It will sell for more if it is obviously unused.
2. If the cycle is used, always check the brakes.
3. Check for punctured tyres. (Repairs are not costly but they are time consuming.)
4. Check that accessories such as pumps, lights, bells, water bottles, etc., are included. (If they are missing your buyer may use this as a way of beating down the price.)

Suppliers

There are bound to be a number of bicycle shops in your area selling new and used bicycles, plus numerous second hand shops and car boot sales where it may be possible to purchase them. However, at trade warehouses it is possible to buy small, medium or large quantities of bicycles at discount prices, at a fraction of what the general High Street retailers could offer them at. Towsure Leisure, 151-183 Holme Lane, Sheffield S6 4JR Tel: 0114 250 3000 Stocks: Cycles at discount prices.

Copywriting
How To Make Money From Writing Sales Copy

It's often said that everyone has at least one book in them. Whether or not this is true, is open to debate, but it's certainly the case that many of us would like to write for a living. The attraction is obvious. You're your own boss, working on interesting creative work, and there's always the chance of untold riches if your work really takes off. For most though the reality is somewhat different. Rejection slips pour down on the doorstep like confetti. All the hard work is wasted. The plain truth is this - the vast majority of people who put pen to paper make nothing at all.

While there is an intrinsic pleasure in writing, we all have to pay the bills. Wouldn't you rather have the enjoyment and the money?

There's one branch of writing which allows you to do just that: copywriting.

The highest paid form of writing

It's a little known fact that copywriters are amongst the most highly paid writers. They may not compete with the Jeffrey Archers of this world in terms of overall income, but if you compare the earnings per word written, no other form of writing even comes close. In short, copywriters get paid more money for less work than practically any other writer. So what exactly do they do?

Salesmanship in print

Copywriting has been called 'salesmanship in print' and that's a fairly good description. Now before you reel back in horror at that word 'sales', you can be reassured: you don't need to be a good sales person to be a good copywriter. Many of the great copywriters couldn't sell a glass of water to a man dying of thirst.... in a face to face situation! But give them a clean sheet of paper and time to think, and they'll write words which sell. That's the goal of copywriting.... to create sales. It might be through a newspaper advertisement, a direct mail piece (sometimes unfairly called junk mail) a product brochure, a TV/Radio commercial, a press release or whatever. The common thread which runs through all copywriting work is this objective: to have a positive effect and to sell!

Copywriters are well paid for a number of reasons. Copywriting as a skill is rarely taught properly - if at all. As a result, competent copywriters are in short supply, and the really good ones are either impossible to find or prohibitively expensive. The demand is massive and growing.

Markets have never been more competitive. Every company needs to sell its products and services, and will always be on the lookout for that all important 'edge'. They all need and can benefit from effective copywriting to enhance their advertisements, sales letters, brochures, commercials and press releases.

For the most part, this task falls to internal staff who have no idea what they're doing, or why. Alternatively, an advertising agency is given the job, who promptly pass all but the most prestigious work on to a junior member of staff. The result? Well, you've probably seen for yourself.

It's open to all
The world of freelance copywriting is open to just about everyone, irrespective of age, sex or education. In fact some of the most successful copywriters had very unsuccessful educational records. Why? The reason is simple: copywriting is like no other form of writing. You can throw all your standard English grammar and parts of speech right out of the window. They just don't matter.

What really matters is communication. Copywrtiting is more like spoken English than written English. Simple sentences, words, and paragraphs are the order of the day. That's far more important than correct grammar, and practically anyone can achieve it.

Lack of good copywriters
The business world is crying out for good copywriters. Or at least it should be! The overall standard is very low. Any company or organisation that communicates with their customers or the public with the aim of selling something (this can be a product, a service or even an idea) is a potential customer for your copywriting service.

Make over £50,000 a year
Many talented writers beaver away for years for little or no reward. Copywriting isn't like that at all. Before you put pen to paper you'll know exactly what you're going to be paid for your work. A fairly average copywriter can expect to earn around £20,000 a year, and a good one around £50,000.

For those who discover they have a real flair, the sky's the limit. Ted Nicholas is probably the world's highest paid writer, word for word.

He charges a minimum of £10,000 to copywrite a sales letter/brochure, and demands five per cent of resulting sales on top. What's more, he has a queue of companies eager to use his services. He turns down more work than he accepts. As a result of this approach he can make as much as £350,000 for writing a single 1,000 word advertisement.

Getting started as a copywriter

At the time of writing, there are no formal qualifications in copywriting. As a copywriter, you will stand or fall by the quality of your work. Potential customers won't be impressed by your qualifications (or turned off by your lack of them!). You will just have to show that you can do the job.

Study as much as you can. There are a number of excellent books and courses available to help you build your copywriting skills, and some of these are listed at the end of this article. Believe it or not, some simple self study of this type will give you a head start on many 'professional' copywriters who rely on little more than instinct.

Copywriting in the form of sales letters, brochures, newspaper advertisements and the like, is all around you. Some examples are good, some not so good. Learn from the good ones, and try to improve upon the bad ones, using what you've learned.

Marketing your service

Once you've reached what you consider to be a good standard, you can start approaching potential customers. Here are just a few ideas to get a copywriting business under way:-
1. Contact all advertising agencies in the area, and offer your services.
2. Contact all graphic designers in the area. They are bound to have clients who also need copywriting.
3. Write to Direct Marketing companies in the area.
4. Contact all companies advertising in your local newspaper.

5. Contact any company sending direct mail to you. You already know they use copywriting.

Every business takes time to build up, and this is no exception. The first few jobs will prove to be the most difficult to obtain, but getting business becomes far easier once you've proved your worth. Most competent copywriters find that they have a waiting list of clients, such is the demand for quality work.

In 1776 Samuel Johnson said that, "No one but a blockhead ever wrote except for money.". While this may be overstating the case just a little, there can be little doubt that getting paid well for doing something you enjoy is very satisfying. If you would like to write for money, and are more concerned with fortune than fame, then a career as a part/full time copywriter could be just what you're looking for.

'Over-heading' for Success

An innovative photographic idea has emerged in the US which requires a little investment, but no previous photographic experience - overhead photography.

Through the use of special, although inexpensive, equipment it is possible to travel around taking overhead photographs of people's property, offices or practically anything. Far less expensive than hiring an aeroplane for the job, there is plenty of scope for commissioned photographic jobs - doing surveys or taking promotional photographs for example. Due to its novelty value, it is also possible to go around photographing people's houses and selling them framed photographs of their property.

There are two types of overhead photographic equipment systems you could use. One is a telescopic mast attached to a car or van with a camera on top and a monitor linkup with the driver, all controlled from the ground. The alternative is a low flying balloon with camera and monitor linkup. In both cases the camera can be easily manoeuvred into position before taking the shot.

The number of applications are endless. People will want photos of their houses and gardens. Companies will require pictures of their head offices, with management and employees standing in the car park. Schools could be photographed with every pupil and teacher standing in the playground outside. Shopping centres, sports events, concerts, festivals, all kinds of sites and buildings can be photographed with this equipment.

High overhead photography means low business overheads. Although you will be on the move constantly, you will be able to claim travel costs back as a business expense, and you won't require the studio or office necessary for other types of photography. Also, you can travel around the country to wherever you are required.

The demand created by the novelty value of overhead photographs should be enough to ensure that your business will be soon (over) heading for success.

Alternative Wedding Photography

Wedding photographers and video operators have become a mainstay of the modern wedding. They offer a professional service, providing the standard shots: taking the vows, cutting the cake, the family group posing, the bride and groom kissing, they provide pictures that can be remembered in the years to come.

Do they really capture the essence of the wedding, the spirit that sparks off the best memories of the occasion? Or to put it another way, have you ever thought that one person's wedding photos look exactly like another's?

The solution to this would be to hire an 'unofficial' wedding photographer, which is a profitable and enjoyable service that anyone with a little photographic equipment and experience can offer.

The alternative photographer or video operator captures all of the off-beat moments which the official photographer cannot cover. From the groom taking a swift nip of whisky before the service and the bride's mother crying happy tears, through to the bridesmaids disco dancing and the best man chatting up the bride's sister at the celebration afterwards, the unofficial photographer captures everything.

Above all, the service provides a unique and personal reminder of a couple's wedding day, and an excellent gift.

Alternative wedding photography can be done by anyone with a camera/camcorder of reasonable standard, who has an eye for a good photo. All they need to do is to be prepared to get to where the action is and record it. You could offer a two-tier service. For £60 plus expenses, you could attend the service and celebration afterwards, shooting perhaps three rolls of film, or one hour of video. This would probably take about three to four hours. Afterwards you would edit the photos and film and hand over the finished album or video.

For a larger fee, you could also cover the stag and hen nights and the homes before departure. It may be a good idea to quote both fees based on taking a fixed amount of photographs and an hourly fee, plus expenses.

Advertise your service as widely as possible, particularly targeting wedding related suppliers such as florists and caterers. Once you have got one order and one set of happy customers, it is likely that this will generate many repeat sales.

The Two Secrets of Mail Order Success

Of all the business opportunities on offer, mail order is probably the most common, and also the least understood. Thousands of people start up their own mail order business every year, and only a tiny percentage experience any reasonable level of success.

Success Or Failure?

There are many reasons for failure: the product, the way it is sold, the back up service, the costing, the list is almost endless. One reason prevails above all others - a failure to understand the two secrets of mail order success. Every successful mail order company uses these, whether they are aware of it or not. By applying these two secrets you will be practically assuring your success.

Secret No. 1 Promotional Expansion

In mail order everything can be tested and responses can be measured. Unlike most other businesses, you can see where your orders are coming from, and what activity has brought them in. This makes life fairly easy. If something isn't working you can simply drop it. The test need cost very little. If something is working - and here's the first secret - you should promote it as widely, hard and long as you can, right to the point where you break even.

Expanding With Success

Many mail order operators find an advertisement that works and make no attempt to expand into other media. Others get bored with a promotion and cut it once responses start to drop off. Wrong! It should be continued for as long as it continues to make money and only replaced with something proven to be better.

Secret No. 2 Multiple Sales

If you are considering starting a mail order business, read this very carefully. This secret alone will make you (or save you) tens of thousands of pounds.

Very few mail order businesses can survive on a single product. Most of the advertisements you see in newspapers and magazines will lose money! That's right, that nice colour advertisement for the scale reproduction of an E-type Jaguar will, in all likelihood, cost the company more in advertising than it will generate in sales. So why place the advertisements?

Lifetime Value

Because the companies know from experience that once they have a customer, he will normally buy something else. That buyer of the scaled down E-type will probably buy a scaled down Ferrari Testarossa later on. Companies talk in terms of the lifetime value of a customer. This can be many times the value of the original sale. More people have gone bust in the mail order business trying to make money from a single product than any other way.

Getting ahead
Take both these secrets into account if you decide to go into a mail based business and you will already be ahead of 75% of companies already in the market.

Reverse the risk
Whether your business is product or service based, you're not going to make any money until people start spending money with you. It is amazing how many people get everything in place - premises, staff, paperwork, accountants, solicitors, suppliers and stock - before they've given a thought to how they're going to pull in the punters.

Here's a sales method which can be adapted to just about any business. It's a system which has proved itself time and time again. Multi-million pound businesses have been built on it and it rarely, if ever, fails. What's more, you probably know all about it.

So what is it? To illustrate how the system works, here's a potted version of a story which marketing guru Jay Abraham uses in his seminars.

The risk reversal method

A man is considering buying a horse for his daughter's birthday. He's narrowed the choice down to two, both of which seem equally attractive in terms of price and suitability. The man decided to go back and look at both animals again before reaching a decision.

The first owner welcomed him back, went over the attributes of the animal again, and restated how it was reasonably priced and just the right size.

The second owner had a slightly different approach. He said the following, "Look, I want you and your daughter to be completely happy with the horse. I don't want you to buy it under any other circumstances, so here's what I suggest. I'll deliver the horse round to your premises this afternoon, together with enough food to last a couple of weeks."

The seller continued, "Let your daughter ride the horse, get used to it and decide whether they're going to get along together. Come back and see me in two weeks. If the horse isn't right for you just let me know and I'll call round and pick it up. No fuss, no hard feelings. If she likes it, as I think she will, bring your cheque book, and you can pay for the horse then."

Which horse do you think the man bought? It's not difficult to guess, is it?

A Technique Adaptable To Any Business

This technique, most commonly called risk reversal, is applicable and adaptable to just about any business. The psychology of it is both simple and strong. The main inhibiting factor in any business transaction is fear of making a mistake.

From Referrals to Riches

When the average person requires a builder, plumber, TV repair man or electrician, it is usually a case of checking the Yellow Pages, ringing up different companies to find out which is the most suitable.

On what basis do we make our choice? On the whole it will be based on who is the nearest, or which firm can provide the cheapest service.

Is the nearest or cheapest service the best? Does the Yellow Pages give details of how good the service is, how reliable it is, what sort of experience the firm has and whether it offers a 24 hour call out service? Generally not, and bearing in mind that in an emergency you will need to sort something out quickly, this is not information that you can find out quickly and easily.

A solution to this problem can be provided in the form of a business referral service. It is a confidential database or listing that offers clients the above information on any number of services in that particular area. Most of your revenue will come from charges placed on businesses providing the necessary information to be included on your database. Because you offer a centralised information service giving callers free information, being excluded from the database will be detrimental to any firms not listed.

Any individuals requiring information from your service will be able to get it for free, encouraging more calls, thus attracting more firms for inclusion. Although it is a feature of the service that people should receive the information for free, you could set up a telephone line charging callers a nominal fee for each phone call.

The types of firms you should include in your listing are all the usual services such as the ones above - you could use the Yellow Pages headings as a guide. You could also include people like nannies, home helps, gardeners, baby-sitters, bodyguards, DJs and home workers.

Any firm seen as being unreliable or expensive could either be listed as such or excluded altogether, giving firms an added incentive to improve their services and/or pay for inclusion. Of course, any firms that are included are likely to get extra custom as a result, so this may guarantee firms paying out fees to be included. As the referral service develops, your customers may recommend firms they have used, and firms included may use your service in their advertising, giving the referral service extra prestige.

Setting up the service will require a little time and effort in research, plus some advertising expenditure, although it is not a business which requires any previous qualifications or experience. Ideally the information should be stored on a computer database, which will allow records to be accessed quickly and information updated easily, although an index card system will suffice.

Once the service is established, the running costs should be very low and less advertising will be necessary. Updating the service is easy, as firms and callers alike will be eager to provide information. As a result, with little time, expense and effort on your part, the referral service can provide a significant income.

Push Button Profits
The Dedicated Telephone Service

How utilising modern technology and setting up a dedicated telephone line service in hotels, clubs and other places can earn you big money.

Modern push-button telephones have many advantages over the old circular dial phones. Not only are they easier to use, but due to the wonders of modern technology, they can be pre-programmed; give you the number of the previous caller and even screen your calls.

A new business opportunity utilises the technology of modern telephones. They can be pre-programmed to call up any number of services, according to their location.

The basic idea is to set up dedicated phone lines in hotels, clubs and other places, with single numbers programmed for different services. When a person books into a hotel room after a hard days travelling, on finding they are in need of a particular service, they do not want the hassle of searching through telephone directories to find what they want. How much easier just to press a number on the phone and instantly call up what they require.

The idea works by approaching various services likely to be required by people in the hotel. These companies then pay a fee in order to have their own exclusive direct number on the telephone and be the sole provider of that service.

The types of companies that would pay to be included are taxis, car hire companies, travel agents, ticket booking entertainment agencies, laundry and dry-cleaning services, mobile hairdressers and make up people, accommodation brokers, escort agencies and probably many more.

Start by looking into the technology necessary to provide the service, although it may be that the hotel phones already have that technology. You will then need to approach hotels with a view to setting up the service. They may wish to charge you a commission fee, although when offset against the kind of profits you are likely to make, this fee would be minimal.

At the same time, approach as many different companies as possible who may want to have their own dedicated hotel phone number. You should then negotiate an annual or six monthly contract, with fees paid accordingly.

The phones need not be confined to hotels, pubs, clubs, restaurants. Bus and train stations and even shopping centres could all have their own dedicated telephone line service, possibly with different services provided.

Since this is such a simple idea, and since modern technology allows for the easy setting up of lines, this idea represents a business opportunity that almost anyone can try, and should soon become very popular.

Set up a Discount Travel Agency at Home

The prospect of running your own travel business - dealing with exotic destinations around the world on a daily basis - is certainly a very appealing one.

Until very recently this was only a business you could start if you had years of experience in the travel trade, and thousands of pounds of capital to set up your shop. Now all that has changed.

The growth of direct selling in the travel trade means that this is now a business you can start easily from home. All you need is a little working space, a telephone, and the right contacts and you can be up and running in just a few days!

Here we examine just how practical it is and provide the basic background information you need to set up in the travel trade.

Getting Started

Even if you're working from home, you should be professional at all times. No one will want to leave their important travel arrangements in your hands unless you are well organised and efficient.

You will need a telephone and also an answering machine if you won't always be in the office during the day. A fax machine would also be useful. If you have a personal computer (a PC) and a modem, you will be able to use this to obtain quotes and make bookings more quickly, although to begin with it is not strictly essential.

You don't need any experience, qualifications, or any sort of licence to set up in business. Some travel industry suppliers, such as the 'famous people' package holiday companies, will expect you to be a member of a professional organisation, such as ABTA (The Association of British Travel Agents) before they will supply you on a trade basis. However, you can buy and sell many other services from smaller operators - such as air tickets, hotel rooms, car hire and insurance - without ABTA. In face, discount air tickets are one of the most profitable areas to operate in, so this is a very good place to start.

How To Obtain Cut-Price Tickets
There are two very good reasons for specialising in discount air tickets. Firstly, these are much in demand nowadays. Only the very well heeled and business travellers expect to pay full fare. Everyone else expects, indeed demands, a discount. Secondly, by working from home with only minimum overheads, you can sell your tickets at very competitive prices, and undercut your local travel agents without too much difficulty!

You will need to establish reliable sources for your tickets. This can be achieved by approaching what are known in the trade as consolidators. Consolidators buy tickets in bulk from airlines at incredibly low prices - often 10 per cent or less of the full fare price

- then resell them within the travel trade at a mark up. Even adding the consolidator's mark up, and your profit, you will still be able to sell your tickets at much less than the airline's full fare price, (the price the customer would pay if they telephoned the airline and made a booking direct).

Make contact with a selection of consolidators. Sources of this information are given in the 'Useful addresses' section at the end of this article. You will find that they all specialise in different airlines and different destinations. So, if you want to be able to offer tickets to all the popular destinations world-wide, you will need to build up a network of consolidators.

One further advantage of using consolidators is that they will attend to all the administration and ticketing procedures involved, so you don't need to become involved with this. If you like, they are the 'wholesalers' of the travel trade, allowing you to buy whatever tickets you require from them on an easy, no fuss, cash and carry, basis!

Promoting And Selling Your Agency
Although you may feel it is a disadvantage in not having a 'shop front' for your travel agency, it can in fact be an advantage! Unlike your local High Street agent, you aren't restricted to just operating in your own local area. You can operate nationally, in every corner of the country.

The very best way of promoting your agency is to advertise in the National press. The Sunday newspapers in particular are packed with advertisements from discount operators. These have become the 'shop window' of the discount agent and you really need to advertise there to fully maximise the potential of this business.

It is, of course, much cheaper to advertise your business in the local press, and also magazines such as Exchange and Mart. However, do remember that their circulation is much lower than the National press, so the response they generate is bound to be lower. At the other end of the scale, many discount operators find buying pages on the Teletext service is a successful way of promoting their services.

One point: when advertising you will find it easier and cheaper to focus in on promoting just a handful of popular destinations, rather than trying to print a list of every destination you are able to offer. This is cheaper and will also make your agency easier to run.

How This Business Works
At its simplest, this business just involves carefully matching supply and demand. For this reason, try and get to know each of your consolidators in detail, together with the destinations and airlines they each specialise in. This is much more important than a knowledge of the travel industry as such.

When a potential customer calls in, find out the following:
1. WHERE they wish to travel
2. WHEN they wish to travel
3. HOW MANY people are in the party

The next step is to locate the most economic fare for that journey. You will, in fact, find that there is no fixed fare for any particular destination. Different consolidators price in a different way. Not only according to the destination, but also to how many tickets they need to 'shift' that day. For each enquiry a fair amount of shopping around may be necessary in order to find the best buy and this is of course how, as an agent, you earn your profit.

If you have a PC and a modem, you can obtain fare quotes in seconds simply by dialling into the consolidator's computer. If not, it can be done manually by telephone but is bound to take you a little longer.

Once you have located the cheapest ticket, contact your customer and quote them the fare for the journey they require, after adding a suitable profit margin for yourself. You will, in fact, find that many consolidators are able to quote you a recommended retail price as well, so you can immediately see how much you should charge the customer.

Once the customer accepts your quotation, all you need to do is confirm it with your consolidator. This should normally be done immediately, as fares change daily. Within a few days the tickets will arrive from your consolidator. All you need to do is check them, forward them to your customer, and that's all there is to it!

What Sort Of Profit Will You Make?
The good thing about this business is that there is no fixed profit margin. Your profit margin is quite simply the difference between what you buy at and what you sell at. A shop based travel agent, on the other hand, usually works on a mark up of only 10%.

You can also make extra profits by selling travel insurance, car hire and hotel accommodation in much the same way as other services. These services are also available on a trade basis at very low prices. Since most of your customers will also be in the market for these too, it means extra profit for no extra work!

Finally, remember this, even if you have no intention of competing with Lunn Poly, then as well as running a thriving home business, you will still be able to buy travel at trade prices for yourself, your family, friends and colleagues. What other business offers you that?

Buying Computer Equipment at Auction

How To Get Bargains Like:
* a complete new PC system, boxed with manuals, for £150
* a laser printer for £15

* a flatbed scanner for £15

Buying a new computer and all the hardware, accessories and software that goes along with it can be an expensive business. Much easier on the pocket is to buy second-hand, although it means searching around for the right goods at the right price, and there is no protection given to the consumer once the purchase has been made.

The alternative? Buying at auction. An as 'above board' method of buying cheap new or second-hand computers as you can get. Auctions are a source of amazing bargains.

Where else could you get a complete, brand new and boxed with manuals, computer system for just £150? Or a laser printer for £15? Or a flatbed scanner for £15? Or a new professional spreadsheet program for £10?

If you want to purchase a cut price top quality computer system for your home or business, then an auction is the ideal place to do it. Alternatively, if you intend to buy in bulk for resale, auctions are a great source of inexpensive stock that can form the basis of a lucrative business. Here we outline how to buy cut price computer equipment at auction, and how it can be used as the basis of a business.

Why Are Auctions Best For Bargains?
Most equipment sold at auction is sold at a fraction of the price it would fetch through other sources. This is often because goods are sold off in bulk, and/or need to be sold off quickly because the original owner is in dire financial straits. Auctions are a well respected and time honoured method of turning goods into immediate cash, and are much used by liquidators and Official Receivers, as well as overstocked dealers and individuals looking for fast cash.

A huge factor in the unbelievably low prices reached at auction is the large organisations such as HM Customs and Excise, the Inland Revenue, police, bailiffs and county courts, who sell off liquidation and repossession stock at auctions in bulk. They are looking for an inexpensive and quick method of realising assets, and would rather have the capital quickly then wait for the stock to reach the right price.

The large amount of computer stock bought and sold at auction has led to many auction houses specialising in computer equipment, who are working hard to reduce the doubts of non-trade buyers when buying stock without a guarantee. Although 'buyer beware' remains the usual watchword of the second-hand buyer, these auction houses deal only in reputable stock and often guarantees and warranties will now be part of the deal.

Many dealers make a profitable living through buying auction stock and selling it on. As you might expect, they tend to keep their trade secrets to themselves, and as a result the benefits of buying at auction aren't as well publicised as they might be. Don't forget that auctions are open to the general public and anyone can get themselves a super bargain there.

When buying at auction, you do need to have a good idea of what you're buying, as there's often no guarantee or after sales service. There is usually, however, ample opportunity to inspect the stock beforehand. Bulk lots at auctions will also throw up some amazing bargains that are ideal for buyers and sellers of computer equipment.

How To Bid For Goods
When you have decided to attend a sale, your first step should be to contact the auction house to obtain a catalogue. This will help you plan what to bid for. Make sure you know what you can afford to pay for each item and don't go over budget.

The catalogue will give details on the goods' condition, such as whether it is new, in good condition, sold as seen, and so on, and other regulations including inspection, collection, buyer's premium and VAT, and other terms and conditions. Make sure you read and understand these beforehand! You should also make a prior thorough examination of the goods if possible.

Sometimes you will be able to try out the goods and sometimes this won't be possible, so bear this in mind before bidding. Try not to give away any signs of what you are bidding for to other buyers - it may drive up the price. Sometimes 'sharp practice' goes on at auctions, such as deliberately giving misleading information to other buyers, usually to distract them or drive them away from bidding for a certain item. While not illegal, it is best avoided. Be discreet with what notes you make in the catalogue. It can be a good idea to put false notes next to certain items to throw other buyers off the scent.

Once you have decided what to bid for, it is general practice to register with the Auctioneer's Clerk. They will get you to complete a registration form and issue you with a bidder's number or paddle. When the bidding begins, the auctioneer will suggest an opening price and the bidding will increase at certain increments. To bid, hold up your hand, catalogue, paddle or number, to the auctioneer, who will keep referring back to you to see if you want to carry on bidding. Try not to appear over-enthusiastic and not to start bidding for an item too early - it may drive its price up.

The highest bidder gets to keep the goods, assuming the reserve price has been reached. The goods must be paid for upon the fall of the hammer. Usually, at this point they become the property of the buyer, so it is wise to organise transport/collection prior to the auction. If you are new to auctions, attend some to get the feel of the procedure and start bidding for relatively inexpensive items until you gain confidence.

Buying For Resale
Although auctions offer individuals ample opportunity to buy computer equipment at a bargain price, you could use them as a source of cheap stock for resale. You might see bargains that are too good an opportunity to pass up and start buying them to sell on - the profit margin involved and ease of buying makes it attractive.

This Business Has Great Advantages In That:
You can start for little cost: Your initial investment can be less than £100, and your only other expense will be advertising. As you begin to generate profits you can acquire larger amounts of stock.

You can run the business from home: You will need somewhere to store the goods, but unlike other businesses there are no fixed costs involved such as office, shop or factory space. You could easily use a room at home to demonstrate goods, or even travel to customers' houses to do it.

You can devote as little or as much time to it as you wish: If you wanted to run the business as a profitable sideline, the time taken to visit the odd auction and advertise your stock is pretty minimal. You can do it on the odd free day or evening.

The potential profits are large and the financial risks are small: The worst case scenario is that one misguided purchase will mean that you only break even. You are unlikely to lose money and much more likely to make lots!

You can see that there is much to recommend this business, and you only need a basic knowledge of computers to start making an immediate profit. If, however, you want to become a seasoned dealer, here are some tips:

1. Teach Yourself About Computers
You need to know as much as possible about what you are buying and selling, because this will help with buying, pricing, and what to

do when things go wrong. You will develop an instinct for what to buy and what represents a bargain. It also helps to know about the software, which you can demonstrate to help sell your equipment. Occasionally things will go wrong - usually down to the software and easily sorted out. For example, you may need to reload software that has corrupted or that is causing a clash between different applications and extensions. Such problems can be exasperating to the novice, so it helps to be able to troubleshoot your equipment and cut down the time, effort and stress involved.

2. Have An Expert On Hand

You should do basic troubleshooting yourself, although sometimes this will indicate a problem with your hardware. On these occasions it is useful to be able to call upon expert knowledge to put things right. You certainly should not mess about with the inside of a computer if you don't know what you're doing. When your hardware needs fixing, a local expert should be able to put it right for a small fee, and they are useful for when slightly damaged stock is sold at auction and needs only minimal attention to be put right and sold off at full price.

What To Buy

Complete systems, i.e. computer, keyboard, monitor and mouse: These are very easy to resell, although the profit margin won't be as large as for single items.

Separate complementary items: The most profitable way of selling is to buy gear sold separately and then put it together to be sold as a complete system. Sometimes equipment sold at a bargain price will only be missing accessories like cables, cords and manuals, which can be bought for peanuts and added easily, hence drastically increasing the value of your gear.

Second-hand equipment: As long as you can guarantee it is in good working order, second-hand gear tends to have a much higher profit margin than gear bought as new, which fetches relatively high prices at auction.

Bulk lots: It can be a good idea to buy lots consisting of several identical items, such as five Apple colour monitors. There are potentially high profits to be made and will only attract bidding from other serious dealers.

Older versions: It is in the nature of the computer market that hardware and software is updated and superseded all the time. Be wary of buying the latest equipment, which might quickly be superseded and lose much of its value. However, it can be a good idea to buy gear that is still fairly recent, but has already been superseded. For example, a couple of years ago Apple introduced its PowerMac range, and the now former top of the range models dropped in price. You would have lost money if you had large stocks of what had - until then - been the latest Macs, although now they can be bought at fairly low cost, but they still have all the basic features and advantages of the PowerMacs and hence have a good potential profit margin.

Selling Equipment
You should have a good idea of who you are going to sell to and how you are going to sell it before you buy equipment. There is no point buying CAD equipment (sophisticated high tech design equipment used by businesses) and trying to sell it by placing a card in a local shop window. Your main method of advertising will be through small ads in local newspapers, so it is best to stick to mainstream items.

The legal aspects relating to what you sell depend on whether you are regarded as a private seller or a dealer. If you only sell the odd piece of equipment through classified ads you will be classed as a private seller, with the same (lack of) regulations and legal comeback on what you sell. If you have ads going into papers most weeks, then you will probably be regarded as a dealer, bound by various consumer regulations (and there are also the tax and National Insurance implications of being in business).

The Goods Must:
Be fit for the purpose: i.e. sold in accordance with what the consumer was looking for. For instance, you should not mislead someone who wants a computer game into buying CAD equipment.

Correspond with the description: Basically, you should not lie or mislead in any description you give of your stock. For example, by listing it as a colour monitor when it only has black and white.

Be of merchantable quality: i.e. you can't sell equipment expected to be in working order, that is actually faulty. However, if you tell the customer about any faults or defects beforehand, they will have no legal recourse afterwards. You will be subject to various safety regulations, so make sure that any equipment you sell is not unsafe.

Buying For A Third Party
If you want to buy and sell large amounts of stock for profit, but don't want to be subject to the legal and financial implications involved in running a business, then an excellent way to avoid this is through buying for a third party. In other words, you are not buying gear for you to resell, but are acting on behalf of another trader who has commissioned you to acquire stock.

You should find a dealer who is looking for more stock but hasn't the time to go out and buy it. Next, make an agreement on what to buy and how much to pay before attending auctions to acquire equipment that matches your brief. In practice, the dealer you are acting for will either give you the necessary funds beforehand, or make payment arrangements with the auction house. You should be paid a basic daily fee, plus a bonus according to the potential mark up on the buying price. This method avoids any personal financial risk, and you could in theory act on behalf of many different dealers. Alternatively, you could have an agreement whereby you buy goods yourself to supply to the dealer. Although this removes the risk of finding a buyer, you'll have to pay any VAT yourself and unless you're a registered trader you won't be able to claim it back.

How To Choose Auctions To Attend

Although specialist computer auctions have their advantages, non-specialist auctions selling miscellaneous lots often yield the best profits, as other traders are less likely to attend, and the people there may be interested in different items.

You Can Locate Auctions From:

General local publications: For example, your local newspaper will list forthcoming sales in its classified section. If one appears, it is likely that they won't solely be selling computer gear, so you should check how much is on sale.

Specialist computer publications: Micro Computer Mart, for example, is a weekly publication with a two page spread listing major upcoming computer auctions. It also gives details of Computer Fairs - although not as profitable as auctions, these are good sources of bargain stock.

Yellow Pages and Thomson directories: These list all the auction houses in your area. Many of them won't actually sell computer equipment, but you'll be able to find the nearest source of auction stock.

Subscription newsletters: Newsletters are a great source of information about auctions, although you will have to pay to take out a subscription. They give detailed information on forthcoming auctions, and some have additional phone and fax information lines.

Official sources: Much of the stock sold at auctions is repossessed and bankrupt stock, which is sold without a reserve price and sold at very low prices indeed. A good way of targeting these auctions is to go through the Yellow Pages to get phone numbers for repossession firms, liquidators, bailiffs, finance companies and HM Customs and Excise, and ask them which auction houses they use. Alternatively, call the DTI's insolvency service on Tel: 020 7637 1110 and ask them for the number of the Official Receiver in your area, then ring and ask them which auctioneers they use.

Auction Houses

There are many large auction houses all over the country who, as well as all kinds of other goods, sell large quantities of computer equipment. You can find these using the Yellow Pages (your main local library will have ones covering the whole country), computer magazines and newsletters. The UKs auction houses are too numerous to list in full - use the methods we have outlined to find them.

How to Set Up Your Own Employment Agency

As the jobs market becomes ever more competitive there is a growing need for the services of the professional employment agent. There is actually a shortage of experienced and qualified employees in many areas of commerce and industry today, despite what you might hear about unemployment. It is the job of the employment agent to overcome such problems and help to find the right person to fill that job.

An employment agency is a desk based business that can initially be run from home on a part-time basis, but also one which offers excellent growth potential. The biggest agencies, such as Manpower and ECCO have branches all around the world.

Anyone can set up this profitable low-overhead operation at home. Here's how to go about it.

How To Set Up Your Agency

This business essentially involves careful and efficient administrative work. To start your agency, you will need a desk, telephone, and an answering machine if you are running the business part-time. A fax machine and computer would also help the smooth running of your new business.

One thing you must have before you start your agency, is an Employment Agency Licence. This is granted by the Department of Education and Employment. Applying for a licence is not a complicated procedure, however, and applicants are not required to have any prior experience or qualifications.

In due course you may wish to apply for membership of a professional organisation such as the Federation of Recruitment and Employment Services (FRES) or the Institute of Employment Studies (IES). This will enhance the professionalism of your agency and allow you to benefit from links with other members. It will also entitle you to a listing in their relevant yearbooks, which can be a valuable source of business.

There are a few legal points to consider when operating this business. Most importantly you should not charge job seekers merely for registering their details, showing them a list of jobs, or arranging an introduction. You can charge them for counselling, preparing CVs and application letters, and so on, although this is a service normally provided by employment consultants rather than employment agents.

Where Do Your Fees Come From?
You may be wondering how you will make a profit from employment agency, given that you do not charge employees for their services. The answer is that your fee is paid by the employer, who is your client, rather than the employee.

Once you have found a suitable employee to fill a vacancy, your client will pay you a fee based on that employee's salary. Typically, this is between 10% and 20%. So on a salary of £20,000 your placement fee would amount to at least £2,000. On executive salaries of £50,000 to £60,000 then you will be entitled to substantially more!

Selecting Your Area Of Operation

Before starting out, it is vital to decide on an area of operation. The employment market is very diverse and it is difficult, if not impossible, to cover every area of commerce and industry.

You are well advised to cover an area in which you have some personal experience. For example, if you have worked in the motor industry, you might establish an employment agency which recruits employees for the motor trade. If you have worked in an office, then an agency recruiting office staff would be a sensible choice. Areas where there is most often a shortage of suitable employees, and hence greatest demand for the services of professional employment agents, include science, technology, engineering, computing and electronics.

Finding Clients

The next step is to obtain clients for your agency. The best way to do this is to telephone companies who may need your services, or better still, write a mailshot to them and then follow it up by means of a telephone call.

The most effective way to convince them to retain you is on the basis of cost saving. Finding new employees for a particular vacancy can be a major drain, not only on the finances of a company, but more importantly, on their valuable time. Your sales pitch should be that using your agency will actually save them money, rather than add to their expenses.

A recent survey revealed that the cost of appointing an executive on a starting salary of £30,000 was approximately £6,000. Up to 70% of this was accounted for by time 'lost' in considering application forms and the interviewing of unsuitable applicants. If you consider that your placement fee for such an assignment would be just £3,000 (assuming a 10% commission) then you can see that your service is a very cost effective alternative.

Your overall aim should be to sign up clients who will use your service on a regular basis. Thus, handling one appointment every six months may be lucrative, but a contract with a large company which appoints 20 or 30 new employees each month (which is by no means unusual) is very profitable indeed.

Filling Vacancies - How To Find Suitable Employees

Once you have signed up your client you can turn to actually filling the vacancy. This can be done by any method you feel is appropriate to the vacancy in question. However, what we might call unadvertised methods are used extensively in the employment agency business.

Head-Hunting And Networking

One of these methods is what is known as 'head-hunting'. This simply involves approaching suitable people who work for companies in a similar line of business to your client and 'poaching' them by offering a better salary package. Another suitable method is 'networking' which essentially involves mailing or faxing details of the vacancy to other employment agencies and asking if they have any suitable candidates for the position.

Advertising Vacancies

If none of these methods are suitable, then you will need to advertise the vacancy in the press. Only use this method if other techniques have proved unsuccessful, since it involves extra costs and may result in a high number of applications from unsuitable people. One widely used 'trick of the trade' to fill a hard to fill vacancy is to advertise the position in a different part of the country and offer the successful candidate a relocation payment. For example, advertising a London-based vacancy in Scotland, or a Manchester based vacancy in Yorkshire.

Dealing With CVs And Application Forms
Incidentally, few employment agencies operate by finding a job for an employee who approaches them, rather than filling a vacancy for an employer. However, once your agency is up and running, you will probably find that eager job-seekers send you unsolicited applications and CVs. These should always be read, because if you can fill a vacancy from file, you will have no search or advertising costs whatsoever and most of your placement fee will be profit!

Sifting through the CVs and application forms that are likely to flood in is a very important part of the work of an employment agent, since it can otherwise prove extremely time consuming for the client. This is best carried out by asking the client for a profile of the ideal candidate for the job, then working through the applications by a process of elimination.

Using Shortlists
In the vast majority of cases the aim of the employment agent is NOT to identify one single suitable applicant for the vacancy. Rather, you should produce a shortlist of the most suitable candidates with a recommendation that these people are interviewed by the client personally.

If your aim is, for example, to produce a shortlist of three or four applicants for interview, then you can again see that there are considerable time and cost saving advantages in using your service. If the client undertakes this work without the help of an agent, he or she may well be faced with reading several hundred application forms and interviewing 30 or more applicants, most of whom prove unsuitable.

By operating in this way the final decision, and most importantly of all, the responsibility of who to appoint always remains with the client. In other words you earn your fee - which becomes payable to you when the applicant accepts the job offer - mostly for your careful and efficient administrative work.

20 Ideas for Sporting Businesses

Sport has always been something of a national pastime. For the great British athletes and sports people down to the Sunday park footballers, casual golfers and armchair fans, sport holds a great deal of importance.

Sport is also something that attracts a great deal of business. It doesn't matter if you hate sport or whether your only contact with it is a game of pool in the pub on a Friday night. It is still something that many different businesses can be based on, that you can start with little or no previous experience or money.

Whether you watch sport on telly, play once a week to keep fit, or whether you have a particular specialist sporting interest, or even if you know nothing at all about it, there are many different sport related businesses that you can easily set up and run.

Here are 20 of the best sport related business ideas:

1. Sporting Breaks and Holidays
People fanatical about particular sports often take holidays to accommodate their favourite sporting pastime. To take advantage of this why not organise sporting weekends and holidays? Golfing, cricketing and snooker playing weekends, for example, are all likely to attract customers. You could offer sporting weekends in practically any sport if you can find the right facilities. You will need to organise accommodation with suitable sporting facilities nearby, such as a golf course, cricket pitch and nets, or a pool hall. You can then offer tuition, perhaps by a sporting celebrity or even by yourself, with time afterwards to ask questions. Work one to one

on technique, and hold full scale matches. Advertise your service to local sports clubs and travel agents and at big sporting occasions such as cricket matches.

2. Sporting Trips and Travel

Big matches in various sports of national importance take place all the time. There are bound to be people from all over England, Scotland, Wales and Ireland wishing to see their national sides, so you could provide a service ferrying people to and from matches. There are also big events in particular sports such as the Badminton Horse Trials, national snooker championships, motor racing and athletic meetings, and the FA Cup Final - the list is endless. You can provide the travel on its own, offering a coach or minibus service, or offer an all inclusive service combining travel with tickets for the event. Another idea is to provide a service taking supporters of a particular team to away matches. Official supporters clubs organise their own travel to matches, although there is no reason why you can't offer a separate service, or even start your own official travel club. By offering discount bulk buy tickets for a number of matches, you can guarantee repeat business and generate loyal customers.

3. Sporting Tuition and Coaching

We have already covered sporting weekends, although you don't necessarily have to provide accommodation and celebrities. If you have a particular sporting knowledge or aptitude why not organise sporting tuition days, weekends or summer schools, either doing the tuition yourself or hiring experienced coaches? An alternative is to offer coaching by mail order. Manuals, audio cassettes and videos can all be advertised in sporting magazines and programmes and sold by post.

4. Rental Service

Buying and renting out sporting equipment is a good business opportunity. Equipment can either be rented out for short periods, such as a night or weekend, or hired out on a semi permanent basis in the same way as TVs and videos. Snooker, table tennis, and pool tables, trampolines, multi gym equipment, fishing equipment, climbing equipment, plus clothing and footwear, are all ideal for a rental service. Also ski equipment hire for school trips.

5. Supporter Gear
Supporters of a particular team, whatever the sport, are usually fanatical about them and will buy practically anything related to their team. Alternatively, an item could be related to a particular sport or sports person. There are a large number of different items you could make and/or sell that are personalised for a particular team/person/sport. Some of the more popular items might be: T-shirts, knitted hats, scarves, gloves, baseball caps, badges, rattles, mugs, kites, rings, rosettes, pillowcases, tie clips, wall hangings. If possible, produce a brochure containing all the available items. To market them, advertise in team programmes, supporters magazines, social clubs, and at supporters meetings.

6. Pictures
Sport related pictures are a good source of income, and you don't have to be a good photographer or artist. If you have photographic equipment you could take and sell pictures of sports grounds and certain sports people and players. You could also approach sports teams and clubs and take/sell team pictures, personal pictures and action shots. If you have artistic talents, then you could do the same thing with pictures drawn or painted by you. Alternatively, you could collect pictures relating to particular teams and people, and sell them as they are, or have them framed. Posters, postcards and slides are the type of things you should collect. Advertise your service as above.

7. Mail Order Memorabilia
Again, supporters of a particular team or sports person will buy and collect anything related to their favourite team or sporting hero. Mail order football programme sales has become successful and you can sell programmes for all sports, or practically anything else, in the same way. Tickets, match reports, special editions of

newspapers, cups, medals, strips, international caps, boxing title belts, title fight posters, cigarette cards and books are all items that sports fans collect. You can even import them, as sports like American Football grow in popularity. It is a good idea to produce a brochure, and advertise your service in team programmes, specialist magazines and supporters magazines, as well as at social clubs and supporters meetings. You may even be able to set up a sporting memorabilia swap and sale club.

8. Videos

Buying, selling or renting sporting videos is a relatively untried business idea. It is possible to obtain videos of all sorts of big sporting events all around the world which people are likely to want to see again. Videos covering virtually any sport are now available, including personal sporting histories, histories of certain clubs, histories of certain sporting competitions, particular sporting occasions, as well as sporting gaffes. It may even be possible to duplicate old sports films and programmes onto video. Again, produce a brochure so that you can sell by mail order and advertise as above.

9. Indoor Sports

As people often do not have the time, inclination or fitness, to go out and play sports, you could make or sell indoor versions of outdoor sports. Indoor golf and croquet are ideal. They will probably need to be scaled down as lightweight versions of the outdoor equivalent. You could market them to businesses as executive golf and croquet sets, sell them to sports and toy shops, or sell them by mail order.

10. Sporting Snacks

Prepare and package snacks, sandwiches and drinks to sell to spectators before and after (and if the authorities allow it, during) big sporting matches and occasions. You will probably attract many customers, particularly when much of the food available at the bigger sports stadiums remains very overpriced.

11. Fishing Gear

Fishing, although rather more sedate than most sports, is a sport nevertheless, and there are various fishing related goods that you could make and/or sell. Fishing flies and lures can be made very easily and sold at fishing tackle shops or by mail order. Wallets and cases for carrying fishing tackle, bait such as maggots, and even fishing rods, can all be made and sold in the same way.

12. Fishing Services

On popular stretches of river or sea front, a mobile fishing tackle service would be likely to do well, saving the ill prepared angler a trip and enabling them to carry on fishing. Another fishing related service you could offer is having fish stuffed and mounted. By charging a price covering the taxidermist's fee, plus a little extra, you could make money by immortalising a fisherman's prize catch, or simply selling them as ornaments to pubs and restaurants, for example. produce a catalogue and advertise in fishing magazines, gift shops and fishing tackle shops.

13. Player Matching Service

A sports player matching service would offer people a good way of bringing together players of particular sports with similar abilities and interests. For example, this service would be particularly useful to someone who plays squash once a week but can't find anyone to play who is of a similar standard. You could produce special application forms, leaving them at sports centres and shops, and charge people a signing on fee. A related idea is to offer a fishing companion service. You could take details of things like availability, transport, interests and skill and match people up for fishing trips and matches. Produce an application form and advertise your service in fishing shops and publications.

14. Caddie Service

A service providing golfers with caddies for the day could be a good earner. You could train up teenagers and retired people as caddies, with your fees covering their wages plus a certain mark up. You could market your service to local golf clubs and also allow golfers to make direct bookings.

15. Sporting Biographies
If you have collected information or have particular specialist knowledge of a sporting personality, then why not write an unauthorised biography of them. Chances are that if you are interested in them, then other people will be too. Alternatively, if you have writing experience, why not personally approach the sports person and offer to ghost-write their autobiography. Another idea is to produce biographical cassettes and videos, perhaps combining commentary on their lives with shots and sound bites of them in action.

16. Column Writing
Another way to make use of writing experience is to write a sports column for a local newspaper, or write reports on sporting events for newspapers, magazines and even radio stations.

17. Sports Fact Service
One way to put any research experience or in-depth sporting knowledge to good use is to provide a sports fact finding service. Programmes such as Grandstand and Match of the Day pay well for particular sporting facts, which might be along the lines of the last time a player scored a certain amount of runs in a cricket match, the last time a particular club reached the third round of the FA Cup, or the last time a runner attained a particular record breaking time.

18. Supporter Cards
A popular item or gift might be to sell special supporter ID cards, showing that someone is a dedicated supporter of a particular football team, for example. You can print these up yourself if you have a computer with desktop publishing software, or else arrange for them to be printed. You could sell these in packs of 20 outside

matches, advertise them in programmes, or get them stocked at supporters shops.

19. Sporting Songs
Supporters of football teams often have their own favourite songs and chants that they sing at matches. Research the current and past favourites and produce cassettes for different teams, perhaps mixing in bits of match commentary and goal celebrations. Advertise your service at matches, in programmes and in sports shops. It is not just football supporters that have their own songs - rugby, cricket, ice hockey and American Football all have their own distinctive songs and chants. You could put together a tape of rugby drinking songs for example.

20. Classified Sporting Ad-Mag
Producing a national magazine of classified sporting advertisements, mixed with advertisements by retailers and manufacturers or sporting goods, could make a very profitable business. You should include sections for different sports, plus general items such as sports and leisure clothing and footwear.

Using Your Driving Licence As A Passport To Profit

Possession of a driving licence proves one thing - your ability to drive. This ability is one way of making money, although you don't necessarily need your own vehicle. The licence itself can help generate cash. Holding a driving licence could be your passport to profit.

Types Of Vehicle Required
Passenger work, such as minicabbing, is one way of earning a living from driving, and another is delivery work. For these you will usually require some kind of vehicle. Your own, borrowed, or hired. Generally, for passenger work you will require a medium range

saloon or estate car, less than five years old and in good condition. Any van or even a large car will usually suffice for delivery work.

There are exceptions, as your transport may be supplied by the company or individual you are working for. There are also ways of earning money from your licence without driving at all.

What Your Licence Entitles You To Drive

A standard driving licence gives you a wide scope in terms of what you can drive and how you can make money. As well as cars you are entitled to drive minibuses and light vans of up to 7.5 tonnes.

A Passenger Carrying Vehicle (PCV) licence is required to drive coaches, while a Large Goods Vehicle (LGV) licence is needed for lorries. The LGV (C) licence is required for fixed lorries with the LGV (C+E) licence entitling you to drive larger articulated lorries with trailers. Driver training is available in order to gain these licences, but this can often be completed in one week. These courses can cost up to £3,000, but it is possible to apply for a Career Development Loan to pay for this. However, a standard licence should give you ample scope for making money.

Insurance, Health & Safety Considerations

You may require additional insurance if you intend to use a vehicle for business, so remember to inform your insurer before you begin. It is necessary for you and your passengers to wear seat belts at all times and it is advisable to carry a first aid kit. Make sure that the vehicle is roadworthy, safe, and that there is nothing inside the car that passengers could injure themselves upon.

The Image Of Your Business

The image you present is very important, particularly for passenger work, so make sure both you and the car are kept clean and well presented. It is wise to service and valet your vehicle regularly. Use your discretion as regards smoking and in-car entertainment such as the radio, but remember that any passengers may object to smoke and loud music.

Advertising For Work

Generally, if you are advertising your driving services, it is best to have some cards printed, which should include your name and a contact telephone number. It is a good idea to invest in a mobile phone if you are wholly car based.

Place your business cards in popular locations such as newsagents, libraries, supermarkets, shopping and community centres, and company noticeboards. If you run a minicab service, place cards in pubs, nightclubs, leisure centres, cafes, theatres, cinemas, stations, shopping centres or anywhere popular with large numbers of people.

Scan newspapers for 'drivers wanted' ads if you are looking for minicab or agency driving work. Keep an eye out for other driving services ads as you will be able to gauge the market and look out for any gaps.

Ways Your Driving Licence Could Help You To Make Money

Passenger Work

Minicabbing

This is the most obvious way of making money from driving. All minicabbing requires is a car in reasonable condition and a knowledge of the local area. There are usually ads from cab firms in the local press seeking owner drivers. Working for a minicab firm enables you to choose your own hours and once you have paid them your weekly radio hire fee you keep all you earn.

Airport Service

A service ferrying people to and from airports can be particularly popular in the summer months. Not everyone has a car and people with a lot of luggage may not wish to travel by bus or train. This service may prove much cheaper to customers than expensive car parking at airports. A car would be suitable for this work, although if you had a minibus you could ferry lots of customers at once.

Driving The Elderly
A service ferrying elderly passengers in remote areas to the nearest town on certain days of the week, or even to local events and attractions, could prove a useful business. By carefully planning your route, you can collect and drop off your passengers door to door, possibly carrying several groups on one day. A minibus would be ideal for this work, although a large car with plenty of luggage space would be suitable.

Continental Trips
With the channel tunnel providing easy access to the continent and the difference in alcohol duties between the UK and abroad, there is a growing market for 'booze trips'. Driving people abroad to pick up duty free goods and cheaper beer and wine can be a money spinner. Remember to take care about dealing with customs on re-entering the UK and do not overload your vehicle.

Chauffeuring And Wedding Hire
These are two specialised areas where running a freelance service can be very profitable. Both require vehicles from the luxury end of the market, which must be kept absolutely spotless. These services will also require you to wear a uniform and be courteous and discreet at all times. It may be possible to run a business combining these services.

Delivery Work

Removals
Anyone with a van can offer a removal service, concentrating on light services such as garage clearances, helping students or working professionals to move, or even ferrying band equipment. The key to making this a success is offering a professional, trustworthy and cheerful approach, which will guarantee repeat

business. It will be necessary to tell each customer in advance the cost of the job, consisting of a fixed hire fee plus a rate for mileage.

Freelance Delivery

Local traders may require a delivery service as it may be too costly for them to provide their own. By securing the business of a number of traders this service should be profitable. By charging each trader a reasonably low price, you will allow them to make a fixed delivery charge to their customers and make a small profit themselves, thus ensuring you get the repeat business.

Agency Driving

Agencies always require drivers for regular delivery work, such as delivering company stock, parcels and newspapers. Often agencies recruit large numbers of drivers across the country for things such as the release of a new record. It is best to get on the books of as many agencies as possible and keep in regular contact, as agencies tend to offer more work to their regular drivers. Be prepared to drive to the other end of the country at a moment's notice, and also be prepared to wait for long periods at a time for work to come in.

Company Delivery

Companies often require drivers for regular or one-off deliveries. Scan newspapers for advertisements or approach company personnel departments directly. Companies may provide their own transport or may require you to provide it.

Delivery Rounds

Delivery rounds include things like milkmen, sandwich delivery and other foods, combining deliveries with a sales element, taking orders on the way round. If you do this for a company you will usually be paid a salary plus commission, although increasingly goods are sold on a freelance and/or franchise basis.

Other Work

Car-Based Businesses

There are a wide range of businesses which you can operate from a car or van. There are a number of goods which could be sold directly or hired out, such as CDs, books, videos, sports equipment, electrical equipment, or even children's toys.

Delivering New Cars
One way of making money if you don't have your own vehicle is through delivering new vehicles. This work can be obtained through car dealers or agencies, looking for reliable drivers with a clean driving licence to deliver new vehicles to their customers.

Delivering Cars For Servicing
Professional people often need their cars serviced, but find themselves without the time to take it themselves, particularly if it is a luxury model requiring a specialist garage tens of miles away. Assuming you can establish your trustworthiness, you can charge a fixed fee plus an additional charge for mileage or for your time. You could offer an extra service for finding the nearest and cheapest suitable mechanic in the area, possibly even negotiating a commission from the mechanic.

Becoming A Driving Instructor
This is another specialised area, for which you must be over 21, have held a clean licence for three years and passed the Department of Transport Driving Instructor course. These courses, costing around £1,100 are provided by the major driving schools and take between six months and two years to complete.

Making Money From Your Licence
You don't necessarily need a vehicle to make money, as anyone with a driving licence can use it as proof of identification. Building and plumbing equipment, cleaning equipment, carpet and upholstery cleaning equipment and many other 'tools of the trade' can be hired using your licence as ID, along with documents such as your passport, birth certificate or bank letter. This could be useful if

you do not have your own transport and wish to raise enough money to hire or even buy a vehicle.

Cash From Computers
15 Computer Related Business Opportunities

Computers, plus the necessary software and peripherals, have never been as affordable as they are now.

If you are considering purchasing one, remember that although it may be costly in the short term, the income you can generate as a result should pay for your hardware many times over and create a hefty profit too! Here are more opportunities from which you can earn cash from your computer. Each can be lucrative on its own, but you may wish to combine two or more of the ideas.

Business Opportunities
1. Customised Form Production
Businesses require standard forms and stationery of various kinds, such as headed note paper, invoices, compliment slips, order forms and delivery notes. Many go without because they don't have the necessary time or expertise, or because going to a printer requires a large and expensive print run. These forms can be easily and cheaply produced using a good quality package such as Microsoft Office, or a desktop publishing program such as Microsoft Publisher or Adobe Illustrator. These are the leading programs, although there are lots of others you can use.

Produce a standard version of each type of form. You can then modify them according to each client's requirements, printing them out using a laser printer.

Begin by studying examples of these forms and produce your own standard ones. You could incorporate companies' existing logos with the document, perhaps placing them within the document using a scanner, or you could create simple company logos for your clients if required.

Market your service to local companies, perhaps by advertising in the local press and business publications. Sending out promotional leaflets is a good idea, as is marketing via the Internet.

When you have more experience you could produce a wider variety of print, such as posters (often used to advertise events like jumble sales, markets, theatre performances and coffee mornings), party invitations, menus and leaflets. Setting up a print shop will attract the general public as well as business clients. A useful hint is to purchase patterned or textured paper specially designed to go through a laser printer - this will make your forms look more attractive and professional.

You could also produce certificates, which are used all the time at school and work, such as for winning a sporting event, reaching a sales target or completing a course. These are easy to produce using WP or DTP software, and you can charge between £1 and £5 per A4 sized certificate. If you frame it too, you can charge more.

2. Letter Writing Service
Letter writing services have taken off massively in the USA and the same could happen here. Different types of letter might be required for different occasions/receivers, but each style of letter tends to use a standard format. Sales letters, complaint letters, payment demands, job and grant applications, even thank you letters - a standard version of each one could be saved on computer and modified according to each client.

Start by perfecting each standard letter - several books are available that outline standard letters for a variety of situations - and save them on computer. Promote yourself to local businesses by advertising in suitable publications, or contact them directly by letter, leaflet or telephone. At the same time contact community groups to generate non business work.

3. Business Card Printing

If you have a computer with a printer and WP or DTP software, printing out business cards is a simple process. Printers and instant print shops can take hours to even days to print them, but it is a service you can perform in just a few minutes.

Make sure that your software has a range of font sizes and typefaces so that you can make each card look a little different. Again, it is worth using specially coloured and textured customised laser printer stationery to provide the personal touch. A suitable guillotine can be had for around £75.

The business market is an obvious one, but this is another service you may want to offer to the general public at markets, boot sales and other public events. Fake business cards make an excellent gift - you could produce fun ones like "Dad's taxi service", "Mum's Cordon Bleu Cooking", or "Best Grandma in the World".

4. Accounts and Spreadsheet Services

All businesses need to produce some form of accounts. For small traders, it will only be necessary to record a few details by hand in an accounts book for tax purposes, but for most businesses it will be far more efficient to produce computerised accounts using a specialised accounts package like Sage, or a spreadsheet program such as Excel.

Computerised accounts are much quicker and more efficient. Important bills like wages, National Insurance and VAT can be calculated virtually at the touch of a button, removing mathematical headaches at the end of the month, and less filing cabinet space is required. A further advantage is that the data can be modified to produce extremely useful management accounts, enabling managers to know how each sector of their business is doing.

Using these accounts packages is easy for someone who is numerate and has basic computer knowledge. So, setting up a service producing computerised accounts on behalf of other businesses is a lucrative and simple to start opportunity, especially if you already have bookkeeping experience.

Aim your service at small to medium sized businesses, preferably ones that don't use computers. It is worth advertising in local newspapers, although posting leaflets (or handing them in, in person) to targeted companies may be a more efficient marketing method. You only need to take on the bookkeeping for a handful of businesses and you have a full time job on your hands!

5. Computerised Expense Analysis
If you're skilled in the financial area you could provide an expense analysis service, helping clients to track and analyse their monthly expenditure and giving them 'what to do' recommendations. It is an essential business service, helping to control cashflow headaches and maximising profits.

Finance packages such as Sage are very helpful, and particularly useful for personal finances, but any spreadsheet or financial software will do. WP or graphics software is also useful to produce reports.

6. Database Handling
Computer databases are a sophisticated way of storing, filing and handling information. Businesses have to file information, like customers names and addresses, details of clients, suppliers or competitors.

Of course, this can be done using a simple filing card system, but the advantage with using a computer database is that huge amounts of records can be stored, found and updated at the touch of a button. So instantly a manager might be able to see how many clients he has got, where they live and what they have purchased in the past. Databases are an important business tool, but a huge number of businesses, perhaps through ignorance or the time or cost involved in setting them up, do not use them.

Offering a database handling service might therefore be a useful money maker. Software like Filemaker Pro or Access is relatively cheap to purchase and simple to use. You could set up databases to handle a company's records, inputting details and producing file reports when required, working either on an in-house basis, or using your own computer to store companies records. Again, newspaper advertising may be beneficial, but targeting and leafleting selected companies will be a more efficient form of marketing.

7. Handling Business Mailings
There are various spin off services you can offer. Database software (as well as some WP and integrated office programs) has a mailmerge facility, which is extremely useful for various reasons. A standard letter could be written and using the database records, details like customer names and addresses could be automatically inserted into key areas within the letter. You can also print address labels: thousands of letters could be automatically addressed according to selected files on the database, saving the time and expense of typing or writing them out by hand. Bank statements and all sorts of promotional letters are produced in this way.

Many companies will wish to promote themselves using direct mail, but won't have the computer facilities or the time to do it. Offering a business mailing production and handling service will therefore be a useful service for you to offer other companies. All you need is database software with mailmerge facilities and a printer that can handle printing large amounts of letters and envelopes/address labels.

The best way to promote your service is to target small to medium sized companies that you think may want to send out large promotional mailings. Send them all a promotional letter to explain your service and telephone them in person to see if they are interested. You can generate valuable customers this way, and they will be able to see the benefits of your service at the same time.

8. Mailing List Supplies
This is another computer database spin-off. Companies very often keep their customer records on database, giving information on where they live and what they have ordered in the past. It is possible to profit from this information by selling customer names and addresses to other companies.

Firms like to purchase mailing lists because they target customers who have demonstrated a willingness to buy a related productive/service. They are an effective marketing tool and are bought and sold for big money. If you already possess a similar list of customers you could make money by selling it as a mailing list to another company. You could also buy mailing lists from all kinds of other sources and sell them on.

Alternatively, you could put together your own mailing lists. For example, you could go through the local Yellow Pages and put all the companies and their addresses onto a database (any other information, such as company size, products, contact names, might be useful too). Then, for example, if a company selling taps wanted to send a promotional mailing to all the local plumbers and DIY retailers, they could come to you and purchase a mailing list, or simply get you to handle the mailing.

Setting up this business is fairly simple and very lucrative. You could sell mailing lists by advertising in suitable publications, but again direct mail may be the most effective way to promote this service. Make sure each mailing list is current, and update them regularly.

9. Address Label Printing

A further database related business is printing address labels. It is extraordinarily time consuming to type out hundreds of address labels or write them out by hand. However, a computer with a printer set up to print out address labels could perform this task in just a few minutes. So why not set up a business charging people for this service?

The necessary computer equipment is not expensive, and address labels suitable for computer printers can be purchased cheaply from office equipment suppliers. Local businesses might form your main target market, so advertise in the local press and business publications.

Alternatively, you could promote your service to the general public, printing off labels featuring their own address, that they can put on letters, Christmas cards and so on. A small address label printing stall could be profitable at flea markets and boot sales.

10. Computer Business Bureau

Some or all of the services described previously could be provided in the form of a computer business bureau. This is a 'one stop shop' for customers wanting things like accounts, spreadsheets, database and letter writing and mailing services, business stationery, form design, and even fax/e-mail sending and web browsing facilities.

One possibility is to set up a High Street shop with computer terminals and associated software and computer peripherals. This is an expensive option, but you will benefit from the high visibility and accessibility of a High Street site. Alternatively, you could set up the same kind of service at home using a single PC, if you wished. The profits would be less, but as long as you are flexible and offer a range of services, businesses and other clients will come to rely on you and you can make money as a result.

11. Killing Computer Viruses

Businesses can lose huge amounts of money as a result of a computer virus getting into their system. This means they will pay big money for people to come and get rid of them. Don't believe that this is necessarily a job for an expert though. Virus killing software is available from specialised software outlets, and is usually easy to use, requiring you to follow a simple list of instructions. Many virus killing programs are available as shareware too, so this service - at which you can earn up to £50 an hour - should be cheap to set up.

12. Selling Business Opportunities

If you've read the whole of this article, you might already be well on the way to setting up this business! You could set up a 'cash from your computer' club, sending out a monthly newsletter covering computer related opportunities, along with advice, case studies, quizzes and so on.

Another option is to develop and market programs covering different business opportunities. You could send out a disk or CD containing word processed files that explain how to set up and run each business, along with standard letters and forms. You could even include a cash flow and profit/loss forecast so that potential entrepreneurs can monitor their income and profits. Market this service by advertising in business publications and newspapers.

Educational Opportunities

13. Computer Teaching and Game-playing Weekends

Organising weekend breaks, where people can learn how to use a personal computer or play all the latest computer games, is an excellent potential earner.

The venue is the first thing to consider - your home will do if it is large enough, or a local community centre or school will be ideal.

You'll need computer terminals and software too, and someone on hand to provide tutoring or offer technical support.

Put plenty of effort into publicising the event. Taking out advertisements or inserting leaflets into local and regional newspapers and magazines is one possibility. Select your publications carefully: computer teaching weekends will appeal more to people aged 30 plus, who perhaps have never properly been taught how to use a computer. Game-playing weekends, on the other hand, will be more attractive to young people. Placing leaflets in shops and handing them to passers by is another good idea.

Charge each guest around £10-£30 per hour. If your first event is a success, then your computing breaks should become increasingly popular - and profitable!

14. Home Computer Courses

If you have specialist computer knowledge it is well worth cashing in on this by providing computer courses. You could tutor people on a one to one basis in your (or their own) home, or set up a computer class at a local school, office or community centre. Devise different lessons that cover subjects like basic computing and programs such as word processing, desktop publishing and computerised bookkeeping.

Advertise locally to attract students. Another marketing possibility is to contact local businesses with the idea of going in to teach staff on a one off basis. Companies often need to train staff but can't afford to send them on a computing course. An in-house tutoring service represents a cost effective alternative.

15. Computer Correspondence Courses

Many people are looking for a hassle free way of learning more about computing. For people who either haven't the time or the available transport to visit a computer class, a computer correspondence course will solve their problems.

Ideally, you should send out your course in monthly instalments, each covering a particular topic. For example, Month A could cover basic computer use. Month B could cover word processing. Month C could cover spreadsheets, and so on. make your course materials as attractive as possible, perhaps by printing them out using WP and/or graphics software, and include plenty of exercises for your students.

Sell your course by placing ads in newspapers and magazines, and/or the Internet. These needn't be specialised computing publications - advertising in local newspapers may attract computer novices. It is a good idea to produce certificates for people who complete the course. You can charge course members upwards of £100 for 12 monthly sections.

Home Safety Service

Hazards in the household are a significant cause of injuries and even deaths to children. Most of these household accidents could be prevented, if only people knew what to look for.

If you've got a keen eye for spotting and handling potentially dangerous household situations there's an invaluable service you could provide: child proofing homes.

The aim is to make the house totally safe for children, inside and out. You check the client's home and surrounding property, noting all the potential hazards, in order to make recommendations on ways to improve safety. You can make extra cash by installing safety equipment and making any necessary alterations. The home safety service costs almost nothing to set up, and will command premium rates from concerned parents and homeowners because of the peace of mind you provide.

Your first step is to get educated. All kinds of books on home safety can be obtained from the library. It is also worth contacting organisations such as the Health and Safety Executive, the Consumers' Association and the British Standards Institute for more information on safety products and standards.

Next, you should make a checklist of all potential hazards and items to check within the home. You must check whether there is adequate:-

* locks on windows and doors
* working smoke alarms
* stair and fire guards
* guards around electrical outlets
* security preventing access to nearby roads
* fencing around garden hazards (pool, pond, etc.)
* locks on cabinets containing poisons, medicine, alcohol and other hazardous chemicals
* protection from sharp objects and corners.

Be thorough when you make your safety inspection and note down any possible hazard, no matter how small, and what you need to do to prevent or minimise it. Also check things like whether furniture, bedding and clothing is flammable, and list all the important emergency phone numbers. When the inspection is complete, go through the checklist with your client showing the work that needs to be done. You can then offer to do the extra work to make the home safe, or at least offer to supply the necessary safety accessories. When the job is completed you can therefore invoice the client for the initial inspection, plus the labour and material cost to child proof the house.

By targeting schools, playgroups and local newspapers with your advertising, you should be able to make this service a hit with parents. But remember they are relying on you: correcting household hazards is not a responsibility to be taken lightly, so check the safety procedures and legal implications with a solicitor before you begin.

Insurance Videotaping
A New Way to Earn Cash from your Camcorder

All too often we blindly put our trust in insurance companies. We expect them to reimburse us when our valuables are lost or stolen, yet we often forget to keep any proof of possession. Sadly, insurance companies often don't pay out fully because the claimant didn't have adequate proof they owned the items in the first place. There's a new service you can offer that will change this state of affairs - insurance videotaping. Already established in the US, insurance videos are being increasingly used in the UK.

Why Clients And Insurance Companies Need This Service

All you have to do is visit households and go through the house recording on videotape and insured possessions, to act as proof that the items exist. Either the householder or the insurance company itself may hire you to do this.

The other advantage offered by this service is when someone puts in a claim for damage, such as from a fire, flood or high wind. The damage can be recorded on videotape to assess the total cost - insurance companies often now require this when a lease owner makes a claim.

Equipment Required

The only equipment required is a good quality video camera and your blank tapes. Once you've bought your camera, and brushed up on your camera work, send out a letter to insurance companies and/or contact them by phone to advertise your service. Also drop leaflets through the letterboxes of homeowners, particularly those in affluent and crime/disaster prone areas.

What The Work Involves
When you are out recording, start by videoing the outside of the property. Then get the owner to take you through the house so you can video the insured items and/or damage. Ensure your camera has a microphone so you can provide a running commentary. When you have finished videotaping, always keep a copy of the videotape in case a dispute arises. Mark the tape clearly with the customer's name, address and date of the taping.

This service is becoming ever more in demand as insurance companies become increasingly cautious. Luckily, the work and marketing are straight forward and the whole business can be set up for less then £1,000.

Make Money From Games, Puzzles And Quizzes
20 Game related Business Opportunities

How many people own a chess set, a game of Monopoly or Trivial Pursuit, or a computer game like Mario? These games have sold in their billions all over the world, and give an idea of the amazing sales potential that games and related products have.

The truth is you don't have to have invented a billion-dollar board game in order to profit. Devising games, puzzles and quizzes for a variety of markets has more modest, but still excellent, money making potential. And, as ever, there are plenty of buying and selling opportunities. You'll find that even if you hate games and puzzles, there are many low cost start up businesses you can set up to take advantage of them.

Here are 20 ideas for easy to start game, puzzle, and quiz related opportunities. Of course, if you have devised the 'next Monopoly', we'll explain how to profit from your invention!

1. Video Games
It's a common sight in busy pubs: someone piling cash into a video game machine in pursuit of computerised thrills and a possible cash win. But the real winners in the long run are the owners of the machines. By siting them in areas where they will generate good custom - busy pubs and clubs, cafes, bars and so on - each machine can generate well over £200 a week, which is split with the site owner. The best way to get involved is by examining the trade press (e.g. Coin Slot magazine) for a supplier which will help set you up as a local operator. This requires signing a contract and making an investment of around £1,000 to £2,500 per machine. Usually it will be up to you to research the best sites in which to have your machines installed. The great thing about coin operated games is that any profits, after giving the site owner their share, are yours.

Once the machines and sites are established, your main job will be emptying the cash box once a week. It is best to invest in a few machines and ensure they are placed in the busiest pubs and public places - check your sites carefully, as re-siting is costly. You must ensure your machines are up to date and in good working order, and should make any repairs quickly. It is best to contact the British Amusement and Catering Trade Association (BACTA) for advice before you invest. Make sure your supplier is a member of BACTA.

2. Second-hand Slot Machines
Many people won't be able to afford the initial investment necessary for a new games machine. However, a more modest profit can be made from buying and installing second-hand machines, which can be purchased for less than £200.

Persuading site owners to install them may be more difficult than for a new model, but you shouldn't have problems providing your machine is in good condition. By spreading your marketing net widely, to include places like company canteens, community and social clubs as well as pubs, you should be able to generate a good return for very little outlay. The best sources for used and reconditioned machines are the aforementioned trade press, along with classified ad-mags such as the Exchange and Mart.

3. Pub Quizzes

Having exploded in popularity over the last decade or so, it is possible to earn a full time income from compiling pub quizzes. General knowledge and trivia quizzes usually have 20 or 30 questions and a tie-break at the end. Other popular subjects are pop music, entertainment, sport and the 1950s and 60s. Try to gauge the difficulty of the questions - they should not be too difficult but shouldn't be too obvious either. Approach the landlords of as many pubs as you can with samples of your quizzes - you can sell one quiz to many different pubs. They often get quizzes through breweries, so it is worth contacting these also. You could advertise on the Internet - customers could download your quizzes directly.

4. Puzzle, Game and Quiz Compilation

The market for original puzzles, games and quizzes is huge. Crosswords, word searches, quizzes of all kinds, word games, vocabulary tests, mathematical puzzles, spot the difference - these are just a few popular forms of competition that appear regularly in magazines and newspapers, who pay well to be regularly supplied with original items. Contact the editors with suitable examples of your work. Either tailor your puzzles to match the publication (for example, send an animal related crossword to Pet Monthly) or try 'general' publications like women's magazines, puzzle magazines and Reader's Digest. The Writers and Artists Yearbook (published by Black) is available from book shops and lists the editors of UK consumer publications.

5. Quiz Games Shows

Radio and TV companies love quiz game shows because they are popular and relatively cheap to produce. A quick check of the TV and radio schedules for the week will reveal an amazing number and variety of quiz game shows being broadcast. The creators of these programmes are paid a lot of money, and if the show has become successful may continue to receive payments for their initial idea. If you have a good idea for a game show format your financial rewards from contacting TV and radio stations may be huge, particularly if the show becomes one of those 'hardy perennials' like Have I Got News For You, Call My Bluff, or My Music. If you are a quiz writer it is well worth approaching radio and TV stations to see if they require specialist questions.

6. Devising Tests

Tests - serious or light-hearted - are used for a variety of reasons. Some magazines feature IQ, creativity, suitability (such as for a job), personality and vocabulary tests, where the reader can test him/herself on a certain subject. Common in men's and women's magazines are 'fun' tests along the lines of "Are you a good lover?", or "How much do you know about your boy/girlfriend?". Devising this kind of test - where a score is awarded according to which answer the reader gives - requires a particular talent, and publications often buy such articles from writers. If you are talented in this area, as well as contacting magazines you could market an employee test to companies, develop tests for business publications (an example might be "Would you make a good entrepreneur?") or even market them via computer companies - they could develop automated tests for a variety of purposes.

7. Designing Computer Games

Computer software companies are always on the lookout for exciting and original ideas for new games. You need to design a 'story board' showing the different characters, settings, moves, methods of scoring, and so on, in your computer game, which generally gives an idea of how the game will look and progress. You may be given a one off payment for your idea if it is original enough. Alternatively, you can negotiate to be paid a percentage of the total sales, which could be highly lucrative if the game becomes successful. Software company telephone numbers and addresses can be found in the Yellow Pages.

8. Setting Up Treasure Hunts

People love challenges in which they can pit their intellect and ingenuity against others to win a prize - just one reason why treasure hunts are often used as fund-raising events by charities, social clubs, businesses and other organisations. People are generally given a list of clues which they have to follow in order to be the first to reach the prize at the end. Devising a treasure hunt requires good knowledge of the local area and an especially keen eye for small but important details. It may take time for you to research questions and a route for the hunt, but once finished they can be sold to many different customers. Try advertising in a local paper, or better still contact suitable organisations directly. Charge around £30 to £50 for each treasure hunt. People will be happy to pay because a good treasure hunt might get 100 entrants, who can each be charged between £1 and £5 to enter, leaving plenty of profit once the prize has been paid for. Another idea is to devise treasure hunt puzzles to boost the circulation of newspapers and magazines, where the clues are hidden in earlier editions. Since every inch of the publication has to be read to find each clue, advertisers and editors love these puzzles and pay decent fees for them.

9. Lottery Fortune Telling Systems

In the National Lottery, since each ball is equally likely to come up, there is no method to statistically boost anyone's chances of winning. There is a market, however, for predicting lottery wins based on astrology, numerology and similar topics. If you have an interest in these areas, you could set up a lottery prediction phone line, or develop and sell astrological/numerological lottery prediction charts. Get customers by advertising in magazines and 'occult' publications.

10. Sale by Lottery

Here's an ingenious way of using a 'game' in order to sell something for far more than you would normally get for it. Let's say you're trying to sell a second-hand car for £500. Instead, you buy a book of lottery tickets and sell them at £2.50 a ticket with the winner getting the car. By selling the tickets at social occasions and/or at busy shopping centres, you can soon sell enough tickets to put you in profit. This technique can be used in all kinds of situations. Be sure to check the legal and tax implications before you proceed though.

11. Clubs, Magazines, Schools and Correspondence Courses

There are big opportunities in setting up games related clubs, publications and schools. Local games playing circles and schools may be lucrative in some areas. You book the venue (this could be a local community hall or someone's front room if large enough) and, for a small weekly fee, people gather each week to play their game of choice. The most suitable games are 'upmarket' card games such as bridge, poker and blackjack, or board games such as chess, draughts, backgammon and Scrabble.

People who enjoy these games often can't find playing partners, so will jump at the chance of joining a club where they can play with fellow enthusiasts. A local game school could work along similar lines, tutoring people in the rules and tactics of certain games. It's up to you whether to focus on one particular game or provide a general selection. Advertise in local newspapers, shop windows and notice boards for members.

Publishing a magazine or correspondence course covering a particular game or puzzle is another idea. Enthusiasts may want to learn more about how to play/devise them, share ideas, skills and tactics, and meet up with possible playing partners. Good examples of potential mail order correspondence courses or magazines include computer games, role playing games, bridge/poker/blackjack, crossword puzzles, chess, board games (perhaps covering a different game each month), and puzzles in general. Sell them by advertising in national general-interest and/or game and puzzle related magazines.

12. Devise a New Board Game

Undoubtedly one of the most lucrative opportunities in the games world is developing and marketing your own original board game. It should be reasonably simple to learn and fun to play, but must be totally different from any established games. Once you have your idea you should obtain patents and trade marks for it - contact the Patent Office for details. The next step is manufacturing and marketing your game. This will be extremely costly, so it is important to carry out market research before this stage to establish the viability of your idea. The main way independent game manufacturers approach retailers is through trade fairs such as the Olympia Toy Fair - large orders can be secured this way. The trade press carries details of forthcoming fairs. If you can't afford the huge investment involved in independent production you could take your idea to an established manufacturer of games (Spears or Waddingtons, for example). If you are lucky you'll be paid for your idea. Sadly, few games are accepted in this way. Potentially a more successful way is to submit your game to a manufacturer through a specialist agency (see Further Information). They will assess your idea and pay you a commission when sold.

13. Role Playing and Fantasy Games

Commanding cult status among those that play them, there is a growing demand for fantasy games and related products. Devising an original role playing game could be a good money maker. It doesn't necessarily have to be a sword and sorcery style game - it could be a simulation of something as 'mundane' as running a business or shop. Alternatively, you could develop role playing games based on biblical stories, being a famous pop/film star, or something even more weird and wonderful. You don't necessarily have to invent a new game - you could buy and sell a range of fantasy games by mail order, getting customers by advertising in suitable publications.

14. War Games

In both model and real life form, war games remain popular with both young and old. There are various ways you can tap into this popularity. You could produce model soldiers, battlefields and other equipment, or buy and sell these items by mail order. War game re-enactment societies exist in many towns and cities - as well as advertising in suitable publications you could target these societies by direct mail. You could make extra cash by renting out the equipment. Many people re-enact famous battles or get involved in fake conflicts by donning army regalia and replica weapons themselves and going out onto the battlefield. There is certainly money to be made from buying/selling/hiring army uniforms and replica weapons. Also, you could organise holidays and courses for people who want to play at being soldiers. The games/subjects might include pursuit, obtaining and transmitting information, defending positions, and physical objectives.

15. Paintball

A more fun, friendly and safe version of war games - paintball has become a hugely popular pastime. It has become a common form of corporate entertainment too, where companies pay for day/weekend sessions as rewards for employees, to keep clients sweet or to build team spirit. There are two ways you could operate. The cheapest method is to purchase suitable paintballing weapons and lease some land (wooded areas and fields are ideal) to put on outdoor events. Target this service at businesses, societies and other organisations - you can charge fees upwards of £50 per person per day. Alternatively, many leisure companies have been successful in setting up indoor paintball warehouses, where people pay a fee and have a set time to blast as many people as possible with their paint gun. Although far more costly to set up, in a town of reasonable size, this should generate huge interest with evenings and weekends being particularly busy. Since you can charge £5 for a half hour session, this could be a profitable venture. Before you start you must check that your equipment is safe and that you have the right insurance cover.

16. Executive Games
One successful market is executive stress relieving games and puzzles. You could either develop new 3-D puzzles yourself, or else buy and sell a range of executive games. Targeting companies by direct mail may prove particularly fruitful.

17. Outdoor Games
Setting up a game stall at fairs, car boot sales, markets and other outdoor events can offer a useful part (or even full) time income during the summer months. Such events normally charge stall holders only a small amount of cash, and if your stall is popular you can earn hundreds of pounds for just a few hours work. Skittles, coconut shoes, darts and hoopla stalls are commonplace at fairs, and the materials necessary for making them can be purchased very cheaply. A more original idea is to build a set of wooden goal posts with a wooden 'goalie' in the middle on springs. Customers could pay £1 for three shots, and if they score each time they win their pound back along with a prize. Every time someone steps up to take a shot you must set the 'goalie' in motion. Of course, not everyone will win, so you'll still make big money, but the game is not so difficult that nobody can win, so a steady supply of customers will be guaranteed.

18. Game Related Products
Take a look at what's hot in the games market. Could you produce or sell a related product which you have given a new angle to? With an original idea and a knowledge of what sells well, you could profit from this approach. One example is to make/sell souvenir chess pieces in eye catching designs at gift shops, or personalised playing cards featuring a particular theme or even a company logo. You could put a new slant on an existing idea, developing a games compendium with a 'strip' theme, or a range of jigsaws with factual

designs, for example. There are all sorts of products you could invent, but take care not to breach anyone's copyright.

19. Games Playing Conventions, Weekends and Holidays

Many people are so passionate about their favourite game that they will travel long distances to meet fellow aficionados, swap tips and experiences, and play the game they love. They'll pay well for the experience, which is why organising games conventions is a good part time earner. Your guests may want to play the latest video games, bridge or another card game, chess, Trivial Pursuit or another popular board game, or a selection of current and classic games. If you throw in food and accommodation as part of the package, you can charge well over £100 for a weekend ticket. Instead of paying a flat fee to your chosen hotel and caterer, you could arrange a deal whereby each party gets a proportion of the ticket proceeds - they may even contribute to the initial marketing costs. The best way to publicise a games convention is by advertising in games related magazines.

20. Games Rental

A good way to keep a party swinging is by having plenty of games on hand. For this reason party hosts will pay well to hire out video arcade games, pinball machines and board games. Used video machines can be purchased for as little as £200, and a selection of board games could be purchased for even less. You can earn this money back in just a couple of evenings - don't forget to charge each customer a deposit. Market your service by advertising in local newspapers, freesheets and shop windows, or better still, link up with local caterers and party supply firms. You could also approach pubs and clubs, who may wish to hire out your games.

Folding Scooters - A New Kind Of Taxi Service

A new, exciting and inexpensive alternative to the standard taxi service looks set to catch on here very soon. Originating from

Germany, fold up scooters may not sound like a profitable basis for a business, but read on.

Being caught drinking and driving in this country means the driver will get a ban (and a possible jail sentence if fatalities occur as the result of an accident). And that's not the end of the driver's problems - when they want to reinsure their car, the premiums for a former drink driver will be sky high.

So, consider the situation faced by someone who has driven to the pub, but because they fancied a drink finds themselves over the limit. Any right-thinking person, unless they could get a lift from a friend, would naturally call up a taxi to take them home.

This could prove very expensive, and the driver would suffer the inconvenience of having to pick their car up the next day. What alternative does the driver have the they don't want to drink and drive - none!

Well now there can be a cheap alternative, in the form of the fold up scooter service, which operates in a similar way to the standard car taxi service.

Here's how it works. The customer - let's say they are in the Dog and Duck at closing time and they've had a skinful - calls up the scooter depot to get a lift home as they are well over the limit to drive. The rider jumps on their scooter and gets to the Dog and Duck in no time at all. Once there, the customer hands them their car keys, the scooter is folded up and placed in the boot, and the driver runs the customer home in their car. When the destination is reached, the driver picks up the charge before unfolding the scooter and scooting off to the next customer.

As a result, there are no drink driving charges and the customer does not have to go back to the pub the next day to pick up the car.

Because the operating costs for scooters are less then for cars, the overall charges will be very competitive.

To you, this is a business that is incredibly cheap to set up and run. All you need is your own fold up scooter, a phone and the correct road tax and insurance. The novelty value, practicality, usefulness and competitive rates involved will make it popular with customers because it is cheap to operate, it should provide a very profitable business.

The first step is to get hold of a folding scooter - they originate from Germany although UK agents are most likely already selling them - contact scooter agents and distributors for details. Next step is to get the correct insurance for driving a scooter and other people's cars - this won't be a problem as chauffeurs require insurance for a similar service. Contact your insurance broker for information. Finally, you will need a means of communication between customer, base and driver. Taxis use two way radios, which you could use if you have a lot of taxis and riders, although if there is just you, then a mobile phone will suffice.

Make full use of the novelty value when you start up this service. There is much to be gained from contacting local media newspapers, TV and radio, to generate maximum free publicity. Also, there are the standard forms of advertising for such a service like local newspapers, magazines and the Yellow Pages, and it is a good idea to have cards printed and leave them in night-clubs, pubs, bingo halls and so on.

Take note of these pointers and you can set up a similar service very quickly. The fold up scooter service has the potential to be a popular, competitive and above all a profitable alternative to the established car taxi service.

20 Health and Beauty Products and Services

Health and beauty has arguably never been more important. More than ever before, in this health and image conscious decade people want to look and feel good.

Physical and mental health is vital: people want to feel better, fitter and live longer. Looking good is a key aspect of everyone's well being - people like to know they look their best - and it can be crucial in relationships and work. We've generated more and better ways of staying healthy and looking good, so there are now many possible products and services you can make or sell that will allow you to make a healthy living.

If you are skilled or have an interest in any area of health and beauty, there are many potential services you can offer. You can even profit from passing on your expertise. Often it is a case of marketing your service in the right way in order to get the customers queuing up.

You don't necessarily need any prior experience or even any interest in health and beauty to make money from it. There are simple products to make that don't require in-depth skill and knowledge, or you could market products on behalf of someone else. Alternatively, there are related business opportunities in marketing and publishing that you can take advantage of.

Here is our guide to 20 low cost, easy to set up, health and beauty related businesses

1. Health & Beauty Business Visits
People stuck at work all week often don't have the time to exercise or get their hair cut. There is a whole range of services that instead of waiting for customers to come to them, could visit their place of work. Keep fit and aerobics classes, for example, could be held before work begins or during lunch breaks. Any hairdresser, manicurist or beautician with transport, could make appointments

through businesses and visit clients in their lunch hours. A travelling gym could be set up in the back of a van or lorry, so that people can work out during work. Contact the managing directors and personnel managers of medium to large companies in your area - you may need to send them some literature describing your service. Once you have your first booking be sure to make future appointments with your clients, unless you have a regular booking.

2. Anti-Insomnia Products

Not being able to sleep is a big problem for many. There are various anti-insomnia products you can produce to help. Herbal pillows are easy to make. These should have an attractive design and be filled with foam and sleep inducing herbs. A range of bedtime clothing could be produced, perhaps smelling of the same herbs. Cassettes designed to help people relax and sleep soundly are another idea, perhaps containing soothing music and/or a relaxation and meditation programme. Special seashells, which when held up to the ear will produce the sound of the sea, could be popular with children. These products could be sold through retailers such as chemists and market stalls or advertised in newspapers and magazines and sold by mail order.

3. Aromatherapy Products and Services

An increasingly popular form of relaxation and mood therapy, aromatherapy, can be used for fun, or alongside more conventional medicines. There is a range of related products you can develop and sell, either through retailers or by mail order. The number one product is the essential oils. These are used as a bath or massage oil, or to create an aroma, and different oils can be blended to treat different conditions. With some knowledge and skill, you could develop your own range of oils from natural products, create your own branding and sell them in suitable health and gift shops. An easier alternative is to buy the concentrated oils wholesale, blending them together and adding water as you wish, to create your own scented oils. You could develop and/or sell related products such as oil burners, scented candles and handkerchiefs too. If you don't want to actually make the products yourself, you could sell a range of aromatherapy products by mail order. Produce a small catalogue and advertise in newspapers and women's health and lifestyle magazines. Writing and selling a postal aromatherapy course is another option.

4. Sunbed and Gym Hire
Through investing in sunbeds and/or gym equipment and hiring them out for people to use at home, you could very quickly get back what you paid. You will also need a phone, somewhere to store the gear and transport. The free delivery and potential for home use will be a big selling point. Charge a daily or weekly fee and ensure that customers pay a deposit. You could advertise your service in local shop windows and newspapers or distribute leaflets door to door. People who use sunbeds and gym equipment are very common these days and you should find that this business is a profitable venture that will not take too much time and effort to run.

5. Herbal Products
Herbal products can be used either as a safe alternative to many modern medicines, or as a way of masking unpleasant household smells. There are a few easy to make low-cost items in the latter category you can make. Your own range of pot pouri (pleasant smelling herbs) can be made very simply by buying herbs and small wicker baskets in bulk and arranging the herbs attractively in each basket. Sell them in suitable shops or at market stalls, car boot sales and craft fairs. Alternatively, try packaging and preparing a mixture of herbs for adding to bath water, or produce small herb bags to hang in the house, car, caravan and so on. As for medicines, a little research in your local library should give you some old fashioned recipes for improving health and curing common ailments and complaints. You could copy these and produce your own range. Another area to try is the herbal drinks market, which is growing fast. Increasingly being promoted in pubs and night-clubs as a trendy alternative to alcoholic drinks, herbal drinks are full of

natural energy and very tasty. Your own blend of natural drinks should go down well with retailers and customers alike.

6. Home Health and Beauty Services

The two most well known forms of health and beauty service where people are visited at their homes are the hairdresser and the Avon lady type of cosmetics seller. These are both potentially lucrative businesses, but there are other businesses that can operate in a similar way - the aromatherapist, manicurist, make up artist, beautician, masseur or masseuse, sun bed operator, chiropodist, wig fitter and cleaner - the list is endless. If you have experience in any of these areas, or can learn it, then consider running a home visit service. Clients will often pay more for a personal service where they don't have to leave their homes, than they would if they had to visit a shop. Such an operation is not necessarily expensive to advertise - local shop windows will usually suffice to begin with. Once you have developed a small client base, word of mouth is usually the best form of advertising, with your satisfied customers telling their friends and generating more custom. Whenever you visit a client at home, encourage them to invite their friends along to watch, take part, and be handed free samples. This will create a good relationship and will advertise your service at the same time.

7. Health and Beauty Schools

If you have a particular kind of expertise in the field of health and beauty, then you can make money from sharing it and educating people at the same time. Setting up a health and beauty school is something that can be started very easily at low cost. What your school teaches depends on your knowledge - it could be hairdressing, make up, dieting or physical fitness - as long as you make sure you are teaching something where you don't need any kind of medical qualification or special licence (you couldn't set up a school of medicine in this way, for example). The subjects listed above are ideal because they are useful to people in developing a career and those looking for a profitable opportunity. All you need to start with is a suitable space - you can rent somewhere if you don't have the space at home - and suitable education and demonstration materials. Write out a syllabus (what the course covers) beforehand and organise what each of the sessions will cover. Ideally, you should provide each person who has completed the course a certificate as proof that they have knowledge of a particular subject. Advertise your service in shop windows, health food shops and in suitable newspapers and magazines.

8. Postal Courses

An alternative to teaching people face to face is to offer a postal course. Sent out in installments (usually monthly), your course can cover each aspect of your subject. The teaching materials you send out could take the form of a printed black and white or photocopied booklet, explaining the lesson with examples and diagrams if necessary, plus a pupil question and answer section. Again, provide those who complete the course with a certificate. This has an advantage in that you can get customers from all over the world.

9. Consultancy

Consultancy is another business that utilises in depth knowledge. You could become a diet consultant, giving advice on recommended diets and perhaps taking people through established programs such as the F-Plan. Alternatively, you could become a make up consultant, advising people on the most suitable make up for their hair and eye colour, skin tone and facial shape. It is a good idea to visit the homes of clients to give private consultations. Again, advertise in suitable newspapers and magazines and in local shops.

10. 'Stop Smoking' Products and Services

Each year in the UK, 3 million people try to give up smoking. Only 3% are successful. There are a few products that you can make and/or sell to capitalise on this market. 'How to Give Up Smoking' books and cassettes are two obvious examples, but a more original idea is to produce a cassette which can be played whenever someone wants a cigarette. It relaxes the listener and takes their mind off smoking. Another idea is to form a 'Give Up Smoking' club. It can be easier to give up if you know other people are doing it too, so the purpose of the club is to make members feel that they are not alone. Hold meetings at different hired venues each night, focusing on developing each member's willpower and using persuasive anti-smoking arguments to help them give up. It could be a correspondence club, with you sending out a monthly (or weekly) newsletter to members. This could feature articles, advice, letters and even advertising. Anti smoking penalty/fine boxes and ashtrays are two novelty products you could produce. The former is a box in which some money can be placed every time its owner smokes a cigarette, and the latter is an ashtray which can be decorated with a cancerous lung or similarly potent anti-smoking message.

11. Health and Beauty Services Agent

Even if you do not have any particular expertise in health and beauty, there is a way of making money from those who do - as an agent. Taking massage as an example, if someone wanted a home massage, instead of ringing around different home massage services in the area, they could contact you first. You would advise on reputable firms offering the service required by the customer and subsequently make the booking. You take a commission on each booking, perhaps charging each masseur an agency membership fee. You could set up an agency concentrating on one particular area or on health and beauty services in general. To be successful it is best if your service is as comprehensive as possible - that is, comprising as many different services as you can sign up with your agency - and cover as wide an area as you can manage. The key to getting services to sign up is the quality of your marketing. If a masseur can see they will get a lot of extra customers through your agency for the cost of a small commission, then they are bound to be interested. Therefore, you should advertise as widely as possible in suitable shops, newspapers and magazines. If beauty services can see that you advertise widely, it will lend your agency a lot of prestige and get more people to join.

The advertising won't be cheap, but the extra trade and commissions will make it worthwhile.

12. Health and Stress Kits

These items are small kits filled with products designed to relieve stress, or alleviate the symptoms of a particular ailment such as a cold, flu or stomach ache. Both kits can be assembled from already existing products and medicines, and then packaged and sold by you. A stress kit, for example, might contain a video or cassette, a hand grip, a selection of herbal relaxation drinks and pills, aromatic oils and so on. This could be an ideal product for business people, so you could market it through the business press and trade magazines.

13. Health Food and Vegetarian Catering

People's tastes are becoming much more health oriented, and the growth in the popularity of vegetarian foods is continually rising, boosted in part by the British beef and other more recent food scares. People now realise that health food does not just mean lettuce and that a vegetarian meal does not consist entirely of birdseed. To take advantage of this demand, you could become a retailer of health food and/or vegetarian products - setting up a market stall is the cheapest option. Alternatively, why not set up a health/vegetarian food catering service. Devise a menu of tasty and imaginative meals and market your service towards organisers of parties, weddings and business functions. You could place menus in the windows of health food shops and distribute them to businesses. You could also develop a lunch time business round - select suitable businesses and take round a selection of healthy snack type foods.

14. Slimming and Exercise Aids and Services

There are many slimming aids and services you can offer to the hundreds of thousands of slimmers in this country, e.g. books, cassettes and videos containing dietary and exercise programmes. Collect together and market a mail order catalogue of slimming books and videos. Things like dietary drinks, food and pills, plus sports and exercise equipment are suitable complementary products to sell. There is scope for developing your own products too - you could create your own dietary foods, a cookbook, devise a diet and exercise programme or write a slimmers' newsletter. Weight loss holidays are another idea - they could be billed as a fun alternative to visiting a health farm. The best places to advertise is in local shop windows and notice boards, local newspapers, women's magazines, fitness publications, and you could contact slimming clubs too.

15. Mail Order Products

Most health and beauty products are suitable for mail order selling: cosmetics, toiletries, books, cassettes, videos, vitamin pills, herbal medicines, self medication kits, dietary aids and foods, and practically anything health and beauty related that is small and hence inexpensive to transport. Produce a catalogue listing your products and prices and leave them in health food shops, sports centres and cafes. Also, consider advertising in suitable publications. To obtain stock, import products or buy them in bulk from a wholesaler and sell them on at a profit. If you can obtain products from your supplier very quickly, you may not need an expensive prior investment - just get it from your supplier following receipt of your customer's order, and send it on.

16. Door to Door Health and Beauty Products

All the products mentioned above are also suitable for selling door to door, like the Avon lady who sells cosmetics. You could sell a whole range of products in this manner. You need transport plus a bag or tray for your products. Try to have examples of each product to hand and demonstrate items if you can. Ideally you should produce a catalogue which can be left with customers so that they can place future orders with you. This service makes an excellent part time venture to run at evenings and weekends, which are the best times to make home visits. Once you have built up a base of regular customers, this can earn a significant regular income.

17. 'How To ...' Products
You could produce a range of 'How To .....' products - books, cassettes, videos and newsletters that explain how to deal with various health and beauty problems and issues. Potential subjects could be how to prepare for childbirth, how to improve the way you look, how to treat children's illnesses, how to deal with back pain, how to cope with terminal illness and how to beat depression.

18. Spring Water
This business has the potential to take advantage of the growth in demand for healthy bottled spring water, particularly in times of drought. You could run a home delivery service of bottled water, similar to milkmen. To advertise, drop leaflets through people's doors and contact them when you do your rounds. Alternatively, negotiate an arrangement with the owner of a natural spring that allows you to bottle and sell their water. Its exclusive and healthy nature should ensure that supermarkets and other retailers stock it. Be aware that there are health and safety issues relating to this industry - you cannot just bottle and sell any old water.

19. Selling Cosmetics and Beauty Products
Because they are cheap and light, cosmetics and beauty treatments/products can be bought and sold very easily and are ideal for importing and mail order selling. The profit margin is high too. A mail order business operating from home or selling door to door could make an ideal first business. The sort of products to sell are make up, beauty treatments such as facial and body scrubs and ointments, and toiletries. You should do particularly well if you stock the more well known name brands, although it will be more expensive to buy. You could tailor your stock to certain specialised markets. For example, most make up products are targeted at people with white skin - why not buy and sell make up for non whites? By importing in bulk (or even manufacturing your own products) you could be very successful as there is a big demand and

a high profit margin. Baldness products could take advantage of a particular niche market.

20. Health and Beauty Pages Directory

A comprehensive directory of health and beauty services in your area - a 'Yellow Pages' of health - could be profitable. The idea is to include every service, and promote the directory, so that it becomes people's main source of information when they wish to order a health and beauty related service. A small attractively produced free booklet or tabloid should suffice, which can then be left in libraries, health food shops, supermarkets, doctors and dentists waiting rooms, sports centres, cafes and bars for the public to pick up. The chief source of revenue for the directory is advertising. Businesses will be eager to advertise if the guide is guaranteed to reach a certain amount of potential customers. Set your advertising rates according to the amount of page space each ad takes up, the position of the ad within the directory, and how many people in total are likely to read it. To get businesses to advertise, send out mailshots to all the health and beauty related businesses in your area, perhaps making a follow up call. Let them know how many people are likely to read your free guide, printing a new updated version as often as necessary. Give each directory an interesting and current feel by including articles and interviews with local businesses to ensure that people pick up each new version, rather than just keeping their original one.

Government Surplus
How To Obtain Goods & How To Profit From Them

Buying and selling top quality government surplus gear is an unmissable money making opportunity for the shrewd entrepreneur. Every year the UK government spends billions of pounds buying equipment and stock for its many departments and ministries, which has to be disposed of once it has served its purpose. It is usually sold off at bargain basement prices, and the healthy retail prices you can charge make this venture extremely profitable.

Think again if you have visions of buying up Chieftain tanks (low mileage, one careful owner) or thousands of fashionable pullovers in any colour you like so long as its green. Not all government surplus is ex-army, nor is it utilitarian in any way. Often it is perfectly ordinary equipment of the type you would find in any supermarket or department store. Given government purchasing specifications, it is usually of premium quality.

A look at the catalogues of some recent surplus sales reveals all sorts of interesting stock - three piece suites, cookers, microwaves, office equipment, cars, power tools, computers and much more besides. Some of it admittedly is used, but equally some of it has never been taken out of the original packaging.

So now you know what government surplus is, here's how to go about buying and selling it...

Finding Out About Sales
You can telephone any government department or public body and ask them how they dispose of their surplus stocks.

You'll find that most government surplus sales are held by an agency or contractor rather than the government department themselves. This organisation will be authorised to handle all disposals, usually in the form of direct sales, sale by tender, and sale by auction.

To the small trader, the best way of buying government surplus is by auction. They offer you the chance to buy small lots at low prices, unlike the tendering system which often requires you to bid for hundreds of thousands of pounds worth of surplus at a time.

The next step is to obtain details of forthcoming sale dates and venues, which are held at depots all over the country on a regular basis. A professional firm of auctioneers will usually be appointed to conduct the sale and you can obtain a catalogue direct from them.

Buying Successfully At Auctions

Once you have obtained sale catalogues for the kind of goods you are interested in, you will be able to decide which sales you want to attend, when and where they are being held, and which lots are of most interest. If you wish to inspect the goods you can usually make an individual appointment before the sale day.

Bidding in surplus auctions is conducted in the same way as any other auction. Anyone is entitled to bid (be sure to register with the clerk and obtain a bidding card before the sale commences) and the amount you have bid is payable by cash or bank draft on the fall of the hammer. Any lots you purchase must be removed from the venue within a specified time limit, which in the case of most sales is 21 days. If you do not want to bid yourself, or are unable to travel to the sale, most auctioneers will accept a fixed bid by post which they will then make at the sale on your behalf. This must be accompanied by a deposit of 25 per cent of the amount you have bid.

Buying Bargains From The Ministry Of Defence

The Ministry of Defence offers some of the best potential for the small entrepreneur. They dispose of huge quantities of equipment and supplies annually. Much of this is non-military in nature, some new or nearly new, offering plenty of scope to be purchased and resold on the civilian market.

MOD sales are administered by the Disposal Sales Agency (DSA). They in turn have various contractors who handle different types of surplus and dispose of them in various different ways, including by auction. For example, clothing, textiles, motor spares, furniture and computers are all handled separately, by different contractors.

How To Profit From Surplus Stocks

Many purchasers use government disposals as a way of bagging a bargain for their own personal use. So, if you are looking for a car, van or truck, computer or office equipment, or new machinery or equipment for your factory, then you may be able to obtain it at a surplus sale for a fraction of its retail value. However, you can see that even greater rewards are on offer when you buy government surplus for resale on the commercial market.

Obviously, the method by which you turn a profit depends to some extent on the kind of equipment and stock you have purchased. All it takes is a little imagination and you could be buying surplus items for pounds and reselling them for hundreds! Here are some suggestions:

* Classified Ads - Good for reselling cars, vans, trucks, etc.
* Market Stalls - Ideal for reselling clothing, footwear, electrical equipment
* Boot Sales - Can be used to resell tools, equipment and spare parts
* Mail Order - Can be used for reselling household goods, linens, textiles, appliances, clothing
* Retail Shops - A possibility if you are buying larger quantities of surplus. Ideal for reselling furnishings, computers, office equipment, camping equipment and so on.

Once you have gained a little experience in surplus sales, then it is very easy to upscale your operation and buy even bigger and more lucrative lots. Many of the larger companies involved in government surplus supply retailers, wholesalers and industry in general, and there is also a lucrative export trade to be exploited. So, as we said at the beginning, this is an unmissable opportunity for the shrewd entrepreneur.

Cash In A Flash - Starting A Photography Business

Photography is a hobby for millions of people, and wherever there is a beauty spot, tourist attraction and holiday location there are usually plenty of amateur photographers snapping away.

It may be a hobby for you, but try reconsidering it. By reading this article you will soon realise that the camera is a versatile piece of equipment that you can use as the basis of a highly profitable business. It is a business where you can literally call the shots, depending on which area you wish to specialise in. For something that can make you a lot of money, photography is also great fun.

Whether you have a camera or not, have plenty of knowledge and previous photographic experience or not, whether you wish to work part time or full time, or whether you wish to specialise in one type of photography or not, there are plenty of ways to make money from your camera.

Getting Started in Business
Once you have your camera and equipment, it will be time to get started. Remember, once you begin to make money you can put it back into the business and buy better quality equipment, enabling you to take better pictures and charge more money for them.

It is essential that you are well organised and present a businesslike image. It is a good idea to get professional letterheads, invoices and business cards printed - these can be handed to any potential customers.

Depending on what you wish to photograph, you may or may not require a studio. It is possible to set up a temporary studio in your own house, assuming you have enough space and suitable lighting, but you should keep the space looking tidy and professional at all times.

You may wish to take a photographic training course before you start. Local schools and further education colleges will almost certainly offer photography classes. Jessops, the national chain of photographic shops, offers a training course, and there may also be courses advertised in photographic magazines.

It may be useful to take out a subscription to one of the major photographic magazines, as they offer photographic tips, advice, equipment news and reviews, new and second-hand ads and ways to get in touch with people with similar interests. Also consider taking out membership with the British Institute of Professional Photography.

Insurance is necessary, as photographic equipment is very desirable to criminals. Household insurance will not usually cover cameras used for business purposes while out on shoot, so take out specialist insurance. To work as a freelance photographer you will need to contact the Inland Revenue, who will send you a tax return form to complete every year. However, any costs such as travel, advertising, the cost of camera equipment and film, and camera maintenance, can all be claimed back as a business expense.

Photography Business Ideas
Here are various ways of making money from photography. You could specialise in one particular area or you may wish to combine them, particularly in the early days while you are still making a name for yourself.

1. School Photography
Schools organise annual photographs of pupils as a way of raising money and updating records. You do not need much experience to take these simple portrait pictures, so consider approaching schools in your area with a view to getting the work. Try to get some idea of what the schools pay other photographers for the work. They will usually already have existing arrangements with photographers, but

if you can offer a lower price, then the schools may use you instead. When the school has agreed to use your services, arrange a day in which you can come to photograph every pupil in the school individually. You could also take photos of class, year and teacher groups, and sports teams. A teacher will usually organise the times when pupils come to be photographed, so all you will have to do is set up your equipment and shoot.

When you get the photographs developed, try to negotiate a bulk discount with the processing company. You will also require cardboard frames and wallets to hold the photos.

Offer the photographs to the school pupils on a sale or return basis - about 65 per cent sales to 35 per cent returns is an average response - with a commission going towards school funds. After completing the session, make sure you arrange with the school a date to return the following year.

2. News Photography

Interesting and newsworthy photographs are always required by newspapers to stand alongside news reports. They usually use freelance photographs for this purpose, or buy in photographs from particular individuals or photographic agencies. This is a service that you can offer, assuming you can demonstrate that you can be in the right place at the right time and take decent shots. It will be necessary to build up a portfolio of photos to show any prospective clients and employers. Try and develop contacts with news reporters who will tip you off when any news breaks, so you can quickly get snapping at the scene of any newsworthy events. Approach newspapers and news agencies, who, if they are interested in hiring you, will ask to see your portfolio. Whether they agree to use your pictures or not, get straight to the scene of any news event and start taking photos without waiting for authorisation. A single photo, if sufficiently newsworthy, could earn you thousands of pounds if syndicated to different newspapers and agencies. When you have built up a relationship with a newspaper, they will call you out on assignments, paying you per photograph rather than by the hour.

3. Trade Photography
This tends to be of a higher standard than news photography, although you will have much more time to set up shots as it is largely studio based. Companies often require good quality product shots for their packaging, or for trade magazines. Similarly, there are many consumer and trade magazines requiring regular supplies of high quality photographs. Try contacting magazines and the product marketing departments of large companies with a view to getting them to use you on a regular basis. Make an appointment to see them, to which you can take your portfolio.

4. Fashion Photography
This is an area of photography which is highly competitive and can be tough in terms of hours, although it is fun and can be very lucrative. Fashion retailers, magazines and designers all require fashion photographers and will either have their own staff photographers, use freelance photographers, or buy in photos when needed. Your portfolio will be of the utmost importance as you will need to demonstrate that you have good technical ability, a distinctive style and an eye for what makes a good fashion shot. Although it is a tough area to get into, the rewards are enormous.

5. Landscape Photography
Taking photographs of attractive landscapes, buildings and places of interest is one of the easiest ways of making money from photography. You could frame and sell the pictures yourself, or sell them to shops and other places, such as pubs. You could take pictures of local beauty spots, churches, bridges, monuments, streets and stately homes - anywhere that is popular and admired by local people. Decide when the best time is to take the photographs. Sun is generally a requirement for a good photo, with morning and evening times providing the best light. Snow scenes are also popular.

Take various shots of your subject, if possible from different angles, and choose the best one. Following that, get some copies made and have them framed - they should be at least 10" x 8". Then approach places who will sell your pictures, such as gift shops, craft shops, home furnishing shops, and even restaurants and pubs. They will probably agree to take them on a sale or return basis, although ideally they will buy them outright. The price you charge per picture should depend on cost, charging £15 to £20 for a standard 10" x 8" picture which will cost around £3 to produce, with shops getting a commission of between 10 and 15 per cent. The more you expand your business, the more popular and better known you will become, and you may be able to take on special photographic commissions.

6. Media Photography

Photographs of media and entertainment events and celebrities are required constantly by magazines, newspapers and the colour supplements. Indeed, some virtually base their sales upon printing candid shots of personalities. Although the general standard of photograph will need to be fairly high, the main requirements is to be in the right place at the right time. Concerts, film premieres, parties, theatre productions, public appearances and signing sessions - all these generate excellent media photo opportunities if you can worm your way into the right position. Once again, your portfolio will be all important, although a good photo will be bought by magazines, newspapers and news agencies alike, perhaps all over the world. When you are starting off why not offer your services on an expenses only basis, which will give you a chance to develop a portfolio?

7. Sports Photography

Photographs of sports people and events are the staple diet of tabloid back pages and sporting magazines. This requires a particular skill as you not only need to get into the right position, but you need to be able to photograph people moving at high speed. You will also need a camera and film that allows for fast, and possible multiple exposure times, as well as a zoom lens. You will often require authorisation to take photographs as this can interfere with the event taking place. Again, develop a portfolio and offer your services to magazines, newspapers and agencies.

8. Property Photography

One possible lucrative photographic opportunity is to take pictures of people's houses and property on behalf of estate agents. An attractive colour photo is an essential requirement of estate agents to sell properties, so they may be interested in employing you to take their photographs. Contact as many estate agencies as possible in your area with the aim of getting a regular order from them - there is no reason why you can't work for more than one. You could offer to take initial photos for free, to give them an idea of what you are capable of and establish a rapport. Stress to the estate agents that slow selling properties should be re-photographed regularly in order to help boost the amount of work. Once they agree to use you, try to establish the best angle to photograph the property from. You need a shot that enhances the property as much as possible, so if the house has peeling paint, piles of rubbish in the garden, or rusty cars parked outside, you should try not to get them in the picture.

Opportunity Knocks

Opportunities appear at the most unusual times, and in the most unusual places. Apart from revealing one of the cutest money making ideas we've seen in a long time, this feature drives home a very important lesson. Keep your eyes and ears open at all times. You never know when opportunity will strike.

New Years Eve is not a time when you would normally expect to stumble across a money making opportunity. While leaving a friend's house slightly the worse for wear, I saw something in their kitchen which took my eye.

They have a five year old daughter. Hanging on the kitchen wall was a tea towel. But it was no ordinary tea towel. Printed on it was around 50 children's drawings, each one around three inches high. The drawings were very special - each one was created by a child, and was a 'self portrait'. Underneath they had each written their name. I'm sure you can imagine that the drawings themselves were very amusing, but can you see what a great keepsake this would be? Can you imagine any parent not buying one? On asking a few questions, I found that the tea towels were not the only things on offer. In addition to a tea towel with the classes' drawings printed on it, you could also get a T-shirt adorned with your own child's individual drawing.

Give this a little thought, and I think you'll start to see the potential. The children themselves provide the artwork. All you need to do is organise the printing of their designs onto the relevant textiles. Tea towels and T-shirts are just two possibilities. There may be all sorts of other items you could print the designs onto.

The sales potential is enormous. We would see the target group as children in the infant and primary school age group. Schools and pre-school groups are the obvious target.

Let's start with a simple example. An individual school will have in excess of 100 children who fall within the relevant age group. Let's say that just 50 participate in any one school. Assuming we have a selling price of £4 - £5 per towel the potential sales are extensive. Your marketing would stress the 'usability' of the product as well as its value as a keepsake. What you should be aiming for here is a minimum of two sales to each parent, one to use and one to keep for posterity. Then there are the grandparents. Most of the children will have two sets - more potential sales.

On this basis, do you think it unreasonable that you could generate an average of two sales per child - between £400 and £500 in revenue? We haven't sold any T-shirts yet! Let's say we sell one T-shirt to every fourth child. It may be more, but let's look on the downside. That would be 12 T-shirts at say £7.50 - another £90 in revenue.

In this simple pessimistic example, we've generated almost £600 from a group of 50 children, and provided them with products which they are absolutely delighted with.

What about costs?
T-shirts and tea towels can both be bought for less then £1 in quantity. Check out the Trader Magazine or Trading Place (both available from W H Smith) for sources for supply. Printing prices vary greatly. Ring round a few suppliers in Yellow Pages. Your marketing costs will be minimal, because you will approach the schools and other organisations directly.

There is one more cost to consider. It is an important one, because it's going to help you persuade the schools and other organisations to participate. As a thank you for allowing you to offer the service you're going to make a contribution to school or organisation's funds from a percentage of the revenue. This gives the school/organisation an incentive to participate, and an incentive to maximise revenues.

Allowing for all costs, you should aim for a net profit of 40 to 50 per cent. So sales of £600 to a 50 strong group could net you in excess of £250 clear profit for very little work on your part.

Where To Go From Here?
Obviously, there is a fair amount of work to be done. Cost up your products and printing before setting your prices. When you have all the details in place, draw up a list of suitable schools and organisations, and approach them directly. Once you've put the

system into operation in one school, ask for referrals. Head teachers in one school invariably know their counterparts in other local schools, and will be happy to recommend you if their school funds have been swelled and the parents are satisfied with the product. The business can be built from there.

Part 3
187 Quick & Simple Business Ideas To Inspire You!

1. Produce Christmas cards which are printed on the front with, for example, "Happy Christmas from the Smith Family". Or, instead of the name "Smith", pick one of the dozens of other popular surnames. Sell packs of these cards by direct mail to people listed in telephone directories.

2. Make money from renting out expensive children's toys. The toys you rent out will include remote control models and computerised games. Use a little van to deliver the toys to customers. The van should have a toy town colour scheme, sirens and flashing lights. Call the van a toy-mobile.

3. Introduce to your region a service which mounts maps for businesses. Keep a stock of local, national and international maps. Mount these maps in a professional manner to suit the wall space available at offices. Send out leaflets about your service to office managers.

4. Bring out a regular publication for ambitious, amateur musicians. This publication might include ads from: i) employers seeking musicians; ii) retailers selling equipment, accessories and supplies; (iii) people selling used equipment. Also print interesting editorial.

5. Design and manufacture kits for making models with cocktail sticks. For example, model churches, castles, windmills, houses, etc. Buy the cocktail sticks in unpacked form in bulk from a manufacturer. Sell your kits by mail order from ads in craft magazines or distribute to model shops.

6. Produce a directory of products no longer made. This directory might include sections on toys, novelties and household goods.

Design the directory for business people and inventors who want to know both what has been made before and what ideas might be revived or modified.

7. Make cotton gloves specially designed for coin collectors. The gloves prevent the acidic grease and moisture on fingers from getting on to coins. Package the gloves and sell from ads in coin collecting magazines or distribute to shops which sell collectible coins.

8. Bring out a correspondence course about how to write cookery books. The course might include information about: how to devise recipes; how to present them in written form and what makes a successful cookery book. Produce a prospectus and advertise in women's magazine.

9. Begin a business which rents out large and expensive astronomical telescopes to householders who want to develop their interest in astronomy. Publicise your service at the local astronomy society and use local advertising to attract clients. Link up with a telescope supplier and get a 10% finder's fee for those people who go on to buy their own telescope.

10. Set up a company which produces a compendium of strip games, for example: strip poker, strip snakes and ladders, strip lotto, strip snap and strip ludo. Sell the compendiums of games by mail order from ads in x-rated magazines.

11. Paint attractive art on rocks to make souvenir paperweights and doorstops. The art might take the form of abstract patterns, traditional pictures or tourist scenery. Call your rocks 'designer rocks'. Add a rubber base to paperweights and a rubber edge to doorstops.

12. Create a mail order business which specialises in selling products which help people sleep. The products you sell might include: sleep inducing cassettes, special bedtime clothing, herbal

pillows and how to sleep well booklets. Company names might be something like 'Sleepwell', 'Sleeptight' etc.

13. Paint on wood, stylish house numbers and names. These painted numbers and names will be an attractive alternative to the traditional names burned into sliced logs. Get your work stocked at shops which sell garden products or household goods.

14. Start a venture which promotes the art and hobby of window painting. On coloured acetate paper have outlines printed for painting pictures by numbers. These acetate sheets are stuck to one side of a window and anyone can paint a picture on the other side of the window.

15. Select one seashell which would be suitable for use as an ashtray, another for a pip tray and a third for a paper clip tray. Put these shells into a single packet and sell as a set of useful household seashell trays. Find shops to stock your packets of seashell trays.

16. Devise and produce a board game which simulates the experience of starting a mail order business. The usual problem of bringing out a board game is the difficulty of getting it stocked at shops. However, a game about mail order can be sold by mail order to business opportunity seekers.

17. Make an income from selling lucky charms door-to-door. Sell, for example: rabbits' feet, horseshoes and four-leaf clovers. Start this enterprise by tracking down trade sources of these lucky charms.

18. Begin a business which buys and sells oil paintings. Buy new paintings from artists and old paintings from collectors and householders. Sell the paintings from: home, a roadside site, a stall at craft fairs, or hire halls for exhibiting all the paintings you have for sale.

19. Start a manufacturing business which is devoted to making doorstops. The doorstops you make might range from humble

wooden wedges to the exotic and unusual. Package the doorstops in polythene bags, staple on a printed card and get them stocked at hardware or gift shops.

20. Decorate everyday objects with pressed flowers. Add an inlaid design of pressed flowers to trays, coasters, jewellery boxes, paperweights, picture frames, wall hangings, desk sets and table tops.

21. Set up a home improvement business which modifies the exterior of houses to give them a Tudor appearance. Your service will include: fitting ornamental oak beams, giving exterior walls a white covering and adding a metal grid to windows.

22. Make wooden 'strip noughts and crosses' games (an item of clothing is taken off by the loser of a game). Drill 9 holes into a small square block and paint on a grid. Next, make 10 pegs and paint on each peg an 'O' or 'X'. Put the grid and pegs into a clear bag and staple on a product name card. Sell to sex shops and mail order.

23. Bring together a range of brass ware ornaments so you can have a stall at craft fairs, antique markets and Sunday markets.

24. Publish a newsletter which has a title like 'Ambitious Person's Way to Wealth' or 'Clever People Don't Work Hard'. The contents of your newsletter might be in a vein similar to Joe Karbo's 'The Lazy Man's Way to Riches'.

25. Set up and run a school of window dressing. Organise one-day or two-day courses or seminars for established shopkeepers who want to learn more about this aspect of their business. Also provide courses for those who would like to take up a career as a window dresser. (Tip: You can run a profitable seminar on anything without knowing the first thing about the subject yourself. You merely pay a percentage of the seminar fee, say 15%, to an expert speaker.)

26. Write and publish a manual about how to make money from property. In the manual include chapters on: buying and selling

land; buying properties for conversion and renovation; investing in property, etc. Use direct mail and mail order to sell copies of this manual to opportunity seekers.

27. Found and run a school of investment. Give tuition to solo students and groups about different types of investments such as shares, gilt-edged securities, unit trusts, USM, antiques, stamps, art, etc. For each area of investment prepare lesson plans and follow these closely.

28. Make a selection of children's prayer plaques: wooden wall plaques which feature popular prayers. The prayers might be painted on, or burned into, the wood.

29. Start a craft business which uses interesting foreign coins to make jewellery. Incorporate coins into pendants, bracelets, brooches, necklaces and earrings. Alternatively, make jewellery which features reproduction coins from the ancient world.

30. Use small seashells strung together to make necklaces. Find a trade source of small seashells and either set up your own production line, or employ home workers. Sell the finished necklaces from a market stall or get them stocked at suitable retail outlets.

31. Produce 'add-one' drama video cassettes for people in amateur dramatic groups. Professional actors and actresses (or even good amateurs) perform a play on video. However, there is one character missing from the video. This character is played by a viewer of the video. The viewer learns his or her part and becomes part of the play at home.

32. Create a folder of sample sales letters for all occasions. The letters might sell; advice, maintenance, products, a service which gives free quotes, etc. Sell these folders by direct mail to small businesses.

33. Earn money from selling gold chain by the inch at public events such as fairs, markets and exhibitions. Gold chain is remarkably cheap to buy in bulk and the mark-ups are huge.

34. Put together your own mail order catalogue of jewellery making supplies. Locate the sources of products by doing the routine work of a mail order trader: write to potential suppliers. Throughout the country there are thousands of craft workers who would welcome a new catalogue.

35. Earn a living from buying gold and silver jewellery from people who need instant cash. Hence, their need for cash is greater than their desire to get a good price. Only buy the jewellery you can quickly sell at a profit. Remember, the precious metal and stone content of a piece is often far below the value you get from selling it as a whole piece, so don't even think about melting down gold, or stripping the gems out.

36. Use fabrics to make soft cases for pencils, spectacles, scissors, bibles, money, and other small items which are either potentially dangerous or need protection. At first make a diversity of products until you discover a product which is popular and profitable.

37. Buy old bibles and hymn books from churches and education authorities. Have the books shredded. Use the shredded pages as stuffing material for 'bible' or 'hymn' pillows, teddy bears and other soft products. Also do 'bible' confetti and stuff bottles to make bottled bibles.

38. Cut out prints and illustrations from old books. Frame the prints and illustrations and sell through a wide range of shops and from a stall at a market or fair. These framed prints and illustrations can also be sold door-to-door.

39. Make leather and wooden souvenir luggage tags. These tags might feature the name of a holiday town and a popular scene. Get your tags stocked at shops visited by tourists.

40. Prepare a mixture of dried herbs for adding to bath water. Invent a brand name for your product like, '(your surname)'s Original Bath Herbs'. Package each mixture of herbs and get them stocked at a variety of retailers.

41. Begin a service which arranges for people to have their original pop lyrics set to music. This service is to satisfy the vanity of lyricists. Offer potential clients a complete, low cost, package. Attract custom to your service by placing classified ads in the music press.

42. Devise quizzes which test a person's vocabulary. Sell these quizzes to a magazine or newspaper on a regular basis. Alternatively, you might do quizzes which test a person's knowledge of a regional dialect. Sell these quizzes to regional newspapers or magazines.

43. Call door-to-door and offer to buy unwanted furniture. Or use local media to advertise your interest in buying second hand furniture. Sell what you buy from free ads in local newspapers, or start up your own second hand furniture shop.

44. Set up a mail order business which sells motorcycle memorabilia. Put together a catalogue of motor cycle memorabilia which includes: videos, films, posters, photographs, books, instruction booklets, old magazines and newspapers, etc. Advertise your catalogue in motorcycle magazines.

45. Start an enterprise which reproduces classic poems on postcards and posters. Also do framed prints of classic poems. Sell these poetry products from a stall in an antiques or craft market. Or get your products stocked at gift or souvenir shops.

46. Produce a cataloguing system for record collectors. This system might consist of a card index box with pre-printed index cards. Each card has a printed section for the name of the artist, record and

record label. Sell this cataloguing system through record shops or by mail order.

47. Publish a monthly audio cassette for one trade such as newsagents, grocers, hair salons, book sellers, etc. Each cassette should give: trade news, management tips, suggestions for improving sales, etc. Organise a direct mail campaign to recruit subscribers to your audio newsletter.

48. Start a newspaper and magazine roadside stand. Ask established newspaper vendors how they got started.

49. Bring out a correspondence course about how to write short stories for profit. Sell this course from newspaper and magazine ads and charge anything up to the average weekly wage (paid in installments) depending on the contents of the course. (Tip: You can write a course about anything without knowing the first thing about the subject. Simply get some books from the library which cover this subject, read them, then rewrite in your own words as a series of ten monthly lessons.)

50. Produce a correspondence course about how to write good poetry. If most poets received a small amount of tuition about how to compose poems their work would improve dramatically. Sell the course by advertising in women's magazines.

51. Begin an enterprise which deals in new and old American and British comics. This business might: 1) sell comics by post from a catalogue; 2) operate a comics of the month club for specialised collectors; and 3) run a comics stall at fairs and antique markets.

52. Write to overseas publishers of English language newsletters and offer to act as the distributor for their newsletter in this country. In your letter to the publishers outline the benefits they will gain if they let you distribute their newsletter.

53. Start a service which cleans wire baskets and supermarket trolleys. Wire baskets and trolleys often spend most of the day on a

dusty floor or outside in a street open to the elements. This combined with the net-like quality of the wire encourage the accumulation of dust and germs.

54. Use wooden jigsaw pieces to make earrings and necklaces. Add a hand painted design to the side of the jigsaw not covered by a part of the picture. Call your goods jigsaw puzzle jewellery. Sell this jewellery from a stall at fairs or get it stocked at trendy shops.

55. Take metal rods and tubes of different diameters and cut into slices. Arrange the slices to make pictures and patterns. Mount these pictures and sell as craft work. Or produce kits for making pictures with slices of rods and tubes. Use mail order to sell these kits to craft workers.

56. Earn an income from writing articles or books about starting a business and making money. Sell the manuscripts to publishers of business opportunity books, newsletters, magazines and newspapers. For a start, the publisher of this book will welcome any manuscripts.

57. Set up a business which produces a quality audio cassette library of nursery rhymes. Alternatively, produce a series of cassettes which feature X-rated versions of nursery rhymes. Sell these cassettes by either getting them stocked at book shops, or starting a monthly club.

58. Compile and publish a monthly bulletin which informs subscribers of poetry competitions they are eligible to enter at home and abroad. Target your campaign at practising poets for recruiting subscribers to this bulletin.

59. Bring out a series of plans for woodworkers, soft toy makers, leather workers and other craft workers. Either sell printed copies of these plans at wholesale prices, or sell the reproduction rights. So now any craft worker or hobbyist can start a mail order business selling plans.

60. Publish a 'Which?'-type of newsletter about newsletters. As the number of newsletters and subscribers is ever increasing, there is a gap in the market for a newsletter which comments on and judges the value of other newsletters.

61. Begin an enterprise which makes model paper products for dolls and dolls' houses. The model products might include: newspapers, money, stationery, serviettes, paper hats, Christmas cards, etc. Sell these products by mail order to doll makers and collectors.

62. Write a non-fiction book which may, for example, be about a hobby. Pay a book printer to produce copies of the book. Sell these books to the people who would be interested in the contents. You might, for example, place ads in hobby magazines.

63. Give personal tuition in your own home on how to write good English. Advertise your teaching service by placing cards in the windows of local newsagents. In your advertising, point out the advantages of taking your course, such as getting a better job and helping children with homework.

64. Start a singles contact magazine or newsletter. Each issue might include both small ads from people looking for partners and editorial to interest single people. Use press and magazine advertising to build up a list of subscribers.

65. Set up a holiday companion introduction service. Your service matches and introduces single people who do not have anyone to go on holiday with. Place classified ads in numerous publications to attract clients. Or produce a publication which lists people looking for holiday companions.

66. Write and publish a newsletter for those who want to start a successful business. The newsletter might, for example, discuss effective ways of: selling, managing, generating ideas, locating suppliers and finding customers. Use your local library service to research these topics.

67. Begin a craft enterprise which turns out wire craft ornaments. These ornaments are free-standing, 3-D objects which consist entirely of wire: the wire makes the outlines. These ornaments might look like aeroplanes, helicopters, men, animals, boats, bicycles or people's first names.

68. Start a mail order business which promotes the craft of making ornaments and models from shaping wire. Design and make up a complete introductory kit for beginners. Include this kit in your catalogue as well as tools, design ideas and raw materials for wire craft workers.

69. Make football rosettes and get them stocked at newsagents and sports shops. Each rosette might be placed in a cellophane packet or polythene bag.

70. Produce a series of storytelling videos. An actor or actress reads classic novels directly to the camera. Hire out these videos by post. For example, a person might borrow videos of an actor reading 'War and Peace', 'Wuthering Heights' or 'Treasure Island'.

71. Start a venture which organises river or coastal boat trips for: business parties, wedding receptions, anniversaries, birthday parties, etc. Your service does things like: organises transport to the boat; books the caterer; hires entertainers and waiting staff, etc.

72. If you can play a musical instrument, earn money from providing background music at: restaurants, pubs, wine bars, tea rooms, hotel breakfasts, amusement arcades or ice skating rinks. Also play during the intervals at theatres or cinemas.

73. Sell copies of theatrical plays by post. Put together a wide range of new and second hand publications and produce a catalogue. Advertise your catalogue in both the theatre press and theatre programmes.

74. Buy and sell second hand compact discs. Buy collections of discs by post and use local ads to find sellers in your area. The discs you

acquire can be sold: by post, from market stall, or get them stocked at local shops.

75. Have a stall which sells fashionable clothes. Your staff might be a full time business working at street markets, or it might be a part time venture which appears at craft and antique fairs.

76. Set up a sheet music of the month club. Each month send club members a selection of sheets of the latest popular songs. Club members will include: musicians who play at clubs and pubs, record companies and keen amateur musicians.

77. Sell by mail order Beatles or Elvis memorabilia. Conduct your own research to discover what memorabilia you can produce yourself For example, reprint photographs and duplicate press cuttings. Also buy goods from collectors and trade sources at home and abroad.

78. Put together a mail order catalogue of children's educational audio cassettes. The cassettes might cover subjects such as spelling, reading, rules of English, grammar, geography, history, etc. Produce some of the cassettes yourself and buy others from cassette publishers.

79. Do your own research to discover the secrets of conjuring. Write a manuscript about your findings and publish it yourself. The novel and sensational nature of this book means you can sell it from ads in magazines and newspapers.

80. Write and record personalised songs. Produce songs for all occasions such as engagements, weddings, birthdays, anniversaries, new births, homecomings and congratulations. Use classified ads in the personal columns to attract orders.

81. Start a craft business which produces gift tags decorated with pressed flowers. Also do similar products like pressed flower bookmarkers. To make a bookmarker take two strips of clear 35

mm film. Place pressed flowers between the strips and tie the sprocket holes together with cotton.

82. Bring out an educational newsletter about 'How to Improve Your Written English'. Each monthly newsletter might be like a lesson. There are only a limited number of lessons, so you can send the same series to different subscribers for many years.

83. Open a school of rock music. Provide classes about different aspects of rock music such as singing, playing electric guitars, writing music and songs, designing stage presentations, etc. Add credibility to the school by paying practising rock musicians to give many of the lessons.

84. Devise and produce an audio cassette course about how to play the drums. Use ads in the music press to sell this course. Or get the course stocked at music shops.

85. Produce kits for schoolgirls to make bead necklaces. Package each kit in a small polythene bag and staple on a printed card. Mount these kits on a rack and get them displayed at newsagents.

86. Design your own brand of baby sling. Buy one of each of the baby slings currently on sale. Study the slings and develop one which is a composite of the best features. Manufacture and package the baby slings. Find appropriate retailers and wholesalers to stock them.

87. Make charming and attractive quilts for babies and children. Make the kind of quilts you would like a baby or child to have. Give your imagination free reign to see what ideas and designs you come up with. When you have finalised a design, go into business for yourself.

88. Turn out knitwear garments for children. Sell the garments from your own stall or through retailers.

89. Embroider attractive designs on ladies' gloves and scarves. Call on up-market retailers and persuade them to stock your embroidered products.

90. Bring out your own range of shawls. Increase the value of your shawls by giving each design a catchy name. Sell the shawls by mail order or get them stocked at retailers.

91. Make charming soft toy ladybirds which can be attached to curtains for decoration.

92. Bring out a selection of souvenir ties. The ties might feature the name or emblem of a holiday resort. Mount the ties on racks and get them stocked at shops which sell souvenirs.

93. Start a mail order business which sells books, booklets and audio cassettes about how to deal with nasty experiences. The nasty experiences covered might include: violence in the home; break up of a marriage; death of a partner; being sacked or failing exams.

94. Use ribbon to make souvenir pictures, for example: yellow ribbon can be used as the beach; blue as the sea; brown and green for palm trees, etc. Or design and produce kits for hobbyists to make pictures with ribbons. Sell the kits by mail order or through craft shops.

95. Make a selection of Balaclava helmets in the colours of popular football teams or the national flag.

96. Produce a series of videos which have titles like 'How to Give Up Smoking', 'How to Relax', 'How to Lose Weight' or 'How to Sleep Soundly'. Sell these videos by direct mail to business people. Or, try to get a leading chain store to distribute them on a national basis.

97. Have your own fabrics market stall and sell ordinary fabrics, rolls of discounted lines and remnants.

98. Earn money from doing alterations and repairs for local dry cleaning services, menswear shops, factories and offices. Visit these places and inform them of your service. Offer, for example, to collect the goods once or twice a week.

99. Produce cardboard, sightseeing, periscopes and sell them at public events. Make the periscopes yourself. Arrange for the card to be printed and shaped. Assemble the periscopes and add two mirrors. Recruit sales people so you can sell these periscopes along the route of the event.

100. Start a knitting patterns of the month club. Each month members of your club automatically receive a selection of the latest knitting patterns. Members select the patterns they want and return the rest. Or compile a top 30 of patterns and send new entries to club members.

101. Begin an enterprise which sells garden gates door to door. On your sales trips, take with you a smart folder which has a large photograph of each gate you are selling. Provide potential customers with a price which includes installation. Your target houses should be easy to spot!

102. Start a home based computer bureau. There are hundreds of business computer programs available such as wages, record files and accounts. Buy and use these programs to provide a computer service to local businesses.

103. Set up a business which promotes the making of lampshades. Lampshade making can be sold as either, an interesting new hobby, or a business opportunity. Produce a mail order catalogue of lampshade making equipment and supplies. Advertise your catalogue in craft magazines.

104. Begin a computerised dating service. Operate this service like a traditional dating service, but hold all your records on a computer and use the computer to aid your search for compatible partners.

Have leaflets about your service printed and place them at shops in your area.

105. Be a sleep consultant. Large numbers of people have difficulty in sleeping at night. This is not usually a medical problem, but can be corrected by using a suitable method or attitude of mind. Provide people in your area with confidential advice about how to sleep soundly.

106. Start a venture which designs and manufactures portable theatrical footlights. Potential buyers of these footlights include: amateur theatre and dance groups, pop and rock groups, children's entertainers, variety entertainers, nightclubs and mobile disc jockeys.

107. Create an enterprise which rents computers to private and business users. The computers you rent out might be new and second hand. Also rent out peripherals such as printers, stands and feeders. Use local media to inform people about your hire service.

108. Buy original computer games programs from home computer enthusiasts. Find these programs by advertising in computing magazines. Produce a compilation of the programs on a master tape. Have copies of this master tape duplicated on cassettes and sell from ads in home computing magazines.

109. Produce a series of low cost audio cassettes which help school pupils revise for public examinations. You might give these cassettes a brand name like 'Personal Revision Cassettes'. Get these cassettes stocked at newsagents and bookshops.

110. Set up a firm which publishes a monthly computer cassette program for home computer enthusiasts who want to improve their program writing skills (e.g. C++, html or web design). Each cassette might give ideas, examples and tips about how to become a better computer programmer.

111. Start a firm which organises educational holidays and weekend breaks for computing enthusiasts who want to further their programming skills. The courses might be held at a bed & breakfast house out of season. Advertise your holidays and breaks in computing magazines.

112. Design and publish diaries for each star sign. The special feature of these diaries is that a star reading is given for each day of the coming year. Have these diaries mounted in a special display rack. Get astrological shops to accept one of your racks.

113. Use luminous paint (the kind used on watches and alarm clocks) to highlight features on natural ornaments such as starfish, coral, colourful rocks, pine cones, etc. Place these ornaments in a UV illuminated display case to illustrate the luminosity. Get these cases displayed at gift shops.

114. Start an enterprise which makes high quality, home-made paper. Sell the paper at a premium for use as: personal stationery, certificates, presentation scrolls, printing paper for manually operated printing presses etc.

115. Bring out a selection of lucky charms which are for hanging from the windscreens of cars, vans and lorries. The charms might be mini horseshoes, rabbits' feet, wooden or plastic number sevens, four leaf clovers, etc. Package your charms and distribute to a wide range of retailers.

116. Begin a business which manufactures kits for making mosaics. Each kit has a pre-designed mosaic and people have to complete it like a jigsaw puzzle. Use ads in craft magazines to sell the kits by mail order.

117. Set up an enterprise which sells greenhouses door to door. Buy the greenhouses from manufacturers at trade prices. Produce sales literature and recruit sales people to sell the greenhouses for you.

118. Start a postal business which rents out war gaming model soldiers and other accessories. War gaming enthusiasts around the nation can use this service to play war games of any size from any period of history.

119. If you have a spare room, take in a lodger, or start a small scale bed and breakfast business. If you choose the latter, either place a sign outside your house which reads 'Bed and Breakfast', 'Vacancies', or advertise in the window of a main newsagent. Currently you can earn £4,200 tax-free from this method.

120. Make money from anatomical charts. Use the charts to: 1) make stylish framed prints; 2) make unusual designs for T-shirts; 3) decorate household products such as wastepaper bins and lampshades; 4) make decorative or educational posters; or 5) make a collection of educational slides.

121. Make decorations for wine bottles. Each decoration is slipped over the neck of a bottle. These decorations are either wood carved or metal engraved with the name of a restaurant or family. Or make floral decorations: the scent of the flowers complementing the bouquet of the wine.

122. Start a craft business which makes unusual table lamps. Each table lamp might feature a stand made of a conch shell or Victorian bottle. If you hit upon a design which is popular, and there are no problems with obtaining raw materials, this can become a full time business.

123. Take up the craft of jewellery making and as soon as you acquire a basic skill, start selling what you make. Begin by sending for a catalogue issued by a mail order jewellery making supplier.

124. Start a mail order firm which sells equipment and supplies to weavers and spinners. An important market for your products will be those taking up weaving and spinning for the first time. Place ads in craft magazines which are directed at this group.

125. Produce souvenir children's height charts which feature postcard type views of local scenery. Or make souvenir suntan charts. These suntan charts have the complete range of skin shades. A holiday maker buys a suntan chart to make a 'before' and 'after' comparison.

126. Put together a postal course which teaches people how to cut silhouettes. The course might include instruction on how to cut all kinds of silhouettes such as landscapes, animals and people. These silhouettes can be framed or mounted to make attractive wall hangings.

127. Start a venture which organises courses about how to build your own house extension or loft conversion. Hold the courses during the weekends at the construction site of an extension or conversion. Or a bed and breakfast house could be hired out of season for a week long course.

128. Begin a craft business which makes either souvenir or normal tea cosies. Find suitable retail outlets to stock your cosies. You might, for example, make souvenir tea cosies for tea rooms and cafes to sell to their customers.

129. Earn money from selling cheap toys door to door. Visit neighbourhoods which have an above average population of children.

130. Learn how to make soft toys with the long term objective of being able to earn money from teaching others. Eventually, teach solo students, classes or use diagrams to teach by post. Also, bring out a postal course which teaches people how to design their own soft toys.

131. Become a calligrapher of poems. Earn money from calligraphy by scribing: 1) poems by commission for poets and sweethearts; 2) classic poems like 'Desiderata', 'Charge of the Light Brigade', etc.,

and selling them as gift products; 3) poems of local origin and selling as souvenirs.

132. If you have the artistic ability, sketch or produce ink drawings of private houses. Get work by calling on households in the nicer parts of town and showing potential customers samples of your work. Also offer customers a framing service.

133. Commission an artist to do a series of designs for saucy postcards. Arrange for the postcards to be printed. Mount the postcards on small racks and distribute these to retailers at tourist resorts.

134. Become a portrait artist and work in a thoroughfare of a shopping or tourist area.

135. Set up an enterprise which publishes a 'Who's Who of Business Opportunities'. Sell advertising space in the publication to business opportunity firms. Use direct mail and ads in newspapers and magazines to sell the finished publication to business opportunity seekers.

136. Open a small private school of art. Employ artists to teach courses about different kinds of art from oil painting to pottery. Offer potential students: holiday courses, individual tuition, and hold classes during the evenings and weekends.

137. Earn money from illustrating personal names in the style of Dickens illustrator, George Cruickshank. Do work at: tourist sites, shopping thoroughfares, fairs, exhibitions, etc. Also do illustrations by post and offer a service which reproduces your work on personal stationery.

138. Found an agency for all artists such as painters, illustrators and sculptors. Provide work for the artists and specialise in contacting businesses which might not have considered using artists. For example, arrange for murals to be painted in staff canteens and at sports clubs.

139. Begin a mail order firm which promotes the collecting of wine bottle labels. Assemble a wide selection of labels and compile a catalogue. In your catalogue also include: starter packs, albums, framed labels, etc. Collect the labels from used wine bottles at wine bars and hotels.

140. Start a business which sells custom designed drinks bars for the home. Operate this business in a similar style to firms which sell fitted wardrobes or kitchens.

141. Put together a direct mail business which sells products to pubs, wine bars and hotel bars. The products in your catalogue might include: books and booklets about making cocktail drinks; quizzes for contests; promotion ideas, pub games, etc.

142. Set up a mail order business which sells equipment and supplies for making herbal drinks at home. This could be an interesting and healthy hobby for anyone to take up. Produce a small catalogue and advertise in a wide range of publications.

143. At a market or craft fair, operate a children's lucky dip. A lucky dip consists of a box full of sawdust mixed with toys in wrapping paper. A child's mum pays a standard charge, for example, one pound, and the child takes out a wrapped toy.

144. If you are familiar with electronics, start a mail order business which sells electronics kits, components and accessories. If possible, bring out your own electronics kits. To obtain other products, get some letterheads printed and write to trade suppliers at home and abroad.

145. Begin an enterprise which makes a wide range of electrical extension leads. Make extra long leads, for people with large gardens; for businesses make industrial extension leads which are up to 1000 feet in length. Get shops and trade suppliers to accept orders for you.

146. Open a school for disc jockeys. Offer potential students different courses for radio, nightclubs, mobile discos, hospital radio and pirate radio. Give students tuition: in classes, on a one to one basis, by correspondence course and through audio cassettes.

147. Earn an income from supplying a fortune teller or numerologist to parties and weddings. A visiting fortune teller or numerologist makes a party or wedding more entertaining for guests.

148. Become a photograph agent. Sell the work of amateur photographers for a commission. As an agent, your knowledge of the best place to sell photographs at home and abroad could lead to some amateurs becoming published photographers.

149. Begin a mail order business which sells folk crafts. Pick a national group such as the Scottish, Welsh or Irish. Put together hampers of craft products which capture the essence of your chosen ethnic group. Have a catalogue printed and advertise it around the world.

150. Set up a postal enterprise which sells signed photographs of celebrities. Solicit signed photographs from celebrities. Or, if a particular celebrity is in demand, offer to donate money to charity if X number of signed photographs are sent to you.

151. Make a toffee of your own design and add a stick to make a toffee lollipop. Get your toffee lollipops stocked at newsagents or sell from a stall at markets, fairs or exhibitions.

152. Set up a school of 'self-selling'. Teach students of your school how to sell themselves and impress. For example: the opposite sex, work colleagues, job interviews, etc. Hold classes; give individual tuition, or teach people through audio cassette or correspondence courses.

153. Start a mail order firm which sells plans, books and supplies to origami hobbyists. Advertise your catalogue in craft magazines.

154. Be a professional family affairs adviser. Just as a careers adviser gives advice on career improvement and development, your service gives advice on improving the future of an entire family. The advice might be about: finance, careers, education, relationships, etc.

155. Design and make leather stamp wallets for philatelists. These wallets are for keeping duplicates and stamps for sale. The wallets might vary in size from the pocket to the desktop. Sell the wallets through stamp shops or from ads in stamp magazines.

156. Begin a mail order business which sells fund raising aids and accessories. For example: booklets about fund raising ideas, bingo calling machines, scratch cards and many others. Produce a catalogue about your goods and send it to clubs, societies, associations and schools.

157. Put together a debt collection training course for small businesses. Every small business is a potential client. A key selling point is that the cost of the course could be quickly recovered from the more efficient collection of debts.

158. Write and publish a book about betting on horses. In the book include details of betting systems and suggestions about how to assess the likely performance of horses. Sell copies of your book to horse racing punters from newspaper ads or by direct mail.

159. Produce a series of audio cassettes about how to stop or reduce vices and bad habits. The cassettes might have titles like 'How to Stop Snoring', 'How to Cut Down on Drinking', 'How to Pack Up Gambling', etc. Sell the cassettes by mail order and through a wide range of shops.

160. Put together a correspondence course about how to become an amateur magician. The aim of this course is to teach people how to do numerous basic tricks. Thus, this is a foundation course for

amateur magicians. Also, sell the products that are required by the course.

161. Package selections of empty matchboxes. Distribute these packets of matchboxes to newsagents to be sold to children who collect matchboxes. Or get these packets of matchboxes stocked at other shops visited by collectors, for example, stamp or modelling shops.

162. Set up a business which produces a selection of novelty packets of seeds for garden weeds. These seeds might have the same appeal as stink bombs. Sell the packets of seeds through gift or joke shops.

163. Set up an enterprise which delivers table flowers on a regular basis to: restaurants, hair salons, dental surgeries, the offices of professional services, etc. Call on these businesses to sell your service.

164. Earn money from selling cactuses door to door. Carry your cactuses in a cinema usherette type tray.

165. Start a craft business which makes a selection of cactus products. These products such as paperweights, book ends, desk sets, etc., have live cactuses growing out of them.

166. Begin a firm which makes concrete, mini models of cows. Each model is painted to look like a real cow. These cows are for gardeners to put on lawns to evoke the atmosphere of the countryside. Get these model cows stocked at as many garden centres as possible.

167. Set up a business which sells garden fountains to up market householders. Produce quality sales literature and advertise in select magazines. Pay professional builders to do the installation work.

168. Buy ordinary plastic model kits of aircraft and boats. Construct the kits and hand paint them in their original colours. Sell the finished models from a stall at fairs and markets.

169. Bring out kits for making relief pictures with wood. For example, a kit for making a rural scene might include wooden pieces cut in the shape of: trees, animals, clouds, buildings, etc. Sell the kits either by mail order to craft workers, or through shops which sell craft products.

170. Start a seasonal business which sells bulbs door to door. This business is best operated by two people: one calls on houses and the other moves a handcart full of bulbs.

171. Sell novelty trays of English soil to expatriates. A home sick expatriate can return to English soil simply by standing in this tray. The principle of this business can be easily applied to any other nationals. Also, stick a tiny national flag into the soil of each tray.

172. Set up a company director exchange service. Your service arranges for one or two directors in different companies to swap places at board meetings. Use the telephone or direct mail to sell your service to businesses.

173. Import specialist magazines from overseas English speaking countries. For example, magazines relating to unusual hobbies or sports. Your task is to build up lists of subscribers in this country. Begin by writing to overseas publishers to ask if they will supply magazines at a discount.

174. Begin and build a weed removal and control round. Operate this round like a window cleaning round. You might do this work yourself. Alternatively, employ teenagers and retired people, and give them a round like newsagents give paper boys a round.

175. Put together a mail order business which sells products that describe the afterlife. For example, produce a series of audio

cassettes which describe exactly what it is like in heaven and hell. Include these cassettes in your catalogue.

176. Write and publish a series of booklets or cassettes about how to make money from flowers and plants. The titles might include: 'Starting a Florists', 'Setting Up a Nursery' and 'How to Open a Garden Centre'. Use ads in gardening magazines to sell the booklets or cassettes.

177. Begin a firm which hires out: window boxes, bottle gardens, exotic plants, tubs of plants and hanging baskets. Your clients will include: offices, banks, pubs, hair salons, restaurants, exhibitions, etc. Also provide your clients with a maintenance service.

178. Learn about flower arranging at evening classes then earn money from teaching others in your own home. Give afternoon classes to pensioners and housewives. A major attraction of the classes is that they act as a social occasion.

179. Set up a production line which turns out mini gardens in bowls and pots. Sell the mini gardens from your own market stall, or find a diversity of retailers to stock them.

180. Design and make herb gardens for the house or garden. Produce the herb gardens in a range of different containers such as bottles, tubs, trays, large pots or hanging pots. Sell these gardens through suitable retailers or by mail order.

181. Devise a selection of scents specially designed for love letters and greeting cards. For example, the scent of roses for love letters and pine trees for Christmas cards. Set up a business which manufactures, packages and distributes the scents.

182. Bring out a range of herbal or hop filled pillows. Make pillows for different functions. For example: pillows which are an aid for people who have difficulty sleeping; siesta pillows for the garden; nap pillows for the living room and pillows which are specially designed for day dreaming.

183. Devise and organise the manufacture of cosmetics for bald heads. The vacant space on a man's bald head is not something which should be covered up, but it is a canvas for an artist. For example, a bald head might feature: wavy lines, a rainbow, sunburst, or a colour to match the eyes.

184. Begin an enterprise which manufactures old fashioned, reliable flypaper. With the current concern about the effect of aerosols on the ozone layer, it is time for flypaper to be revived.

185. Make wooden puzzles for children. For example, brightly painted wooden shapes have to be fitted into the corresponding hole in a block of wood. Or make a flat wooden animal like a dinosaur or rabbit. Cut this animal into lots of peculiar shapes so it is a challenge to assemble.

186 Hand paint pictures or witty statements on small squares of wood. For example, the pictures might feature animals and the statements might be about cooking like 'Oliver Twist's Favourite Kitchen'. Add a magnet to the back of each square so these can be stuck to fridges and other white goods.

187. Set up a mail order business which promotes the hobby of collecting seashells. Bring out a catalogue which has a large selection of seashells, collecting accessories and books about seashells.

Made in the USA
Middletown, DE
19 April 2025